A Blaze... Like a Shooting Star

Alyosha Kumar

(1984-2007)

A Biography

By

Cmde Arun Kumar
AVSM, NM (Retd)

Frontier India

An imprint of

Frontier India Technology

No 22, 4th Floor, MK Joshi Building, Devi Chowk, Shastri Nagar,
Dombivli West, Maharashtra, India. 421202
http://frontierindia.org
https://www.facebook.com/frontierindiapublishing

Curtain Raiser

MY LIFE OF UPS AND DOWNS

IMPORTANT INCIDENTS DATES IN WEEKS

TODAY WE HAD A SHOCK WHEN MR. RAGHAVN SAID OUR BATHS WERE ALTERNATE DAYS AS THERE HAD BEEN NO RAINS. S WE hope it starts raining in the near future.

MY PERSON IN BRIEF

I am normal like all others, with good and bad feelings and I'm also one who does good and bad. Though I'm immensely intelligent, I dor not it designate myself as the best person, who I definitely is has a better personality than myself. Though I don't show affection outside, but have I a soft corner for but some. Those I love, I love truly, with all my heart.

I am reasonably daring quite with a bit of courage. Though I understand people I can't fulfill their needs. That's why I want my money to be used to start a charity form after I'm no more. I also want to donate my eyes

Written at the tender age of 9

Contents

Preface

In Oct 2007, Ms. Ranjana Auditto, a friend and wife of a senior colleague from the Navy, had come down to Pune to share our grief on Alyosha's tragic and untimely death. Her husband, Admiral Auditto, had come to Bangalore to attend Alyosha's last rites but she hadn't been able to make it. She'd known Alyosha, but only as a boy and hadn't seen much of him in his later years. As we talked, and recounted stories from his life, she was so affected and impressed that she told me to write a book on him. She sincerely felt his story needed to be told. At that time I heard her but was in no frame of mind to actually think about it properly.

As time passed and we learnt to cope with Alyosha's loss, I thought about Ranjana's suggestion and started out by writing posts on Alyosha's blog. The reaction from friends and relatives was very encouraging. This gave me strength to continue writing about different aspects of his personality. Another colleague, late Admiral Bansal, who was my Fleet Commander when I commanded INS Rajput, suggested that at some stage the posts could easily be collated into a book. That's how the present biography of Alyosha has come about. Many thanks to Praveena Balakrishna my office secretary who typed the text.

This is not a typical biography. Alyosha's life was cut short tragically and brutally, just when he was about to embark on his adult and professional life. I have no doubt he could have charted out a name for himself in his chosen field of law. Alas, that was not to be. Still there were facets of his extraordinary personality and lessons from his short life, which merit being told: The message of living one's life according to one's convictions and in all honesty, despite the malfeasant environment prevalent in contemporary society. The thirst and quest for learning, for its own sake. Showing compassion and empathy to fellow beings without expecting anything in return. His short life of 22 years and ten months mirrored such qualities. The book accordingly, is not a chronological account of Alyosha's life but focuses on recounting facets of his personality and character. The chapters have been so arranged.

It's extremely difficult and painful to write about one's progeny especially when his life was taken away in such a cruel manner. The perennial grief that comes with it acts as a mental inhibitor. Nevertheless, with perseverance and the support and encouragement of our near and dear ones, I was able bring this exercise to fruition. It has taken some years and some of the content may seem dated, but eventually it has still been worth the while. I sincerely hope that anyone who cares to read this short biography will find it touching and will be able to relate to it.

I must acknowledge all the support and encouragement that were proffered to me to complete this onerous task. My gratitude goes to Ranjana who first egged me on to write Alyosha's story. My deepest gratitude to my wife Deepa for her unstinting support in this endeavour and to my sister-in-law Sabena, who was so helpful in formatting the posts on to the blog and inserting photographs alongside the text, and who has done the same for this book. My siblings, who have stood by me, especially the younger of my two sisters, Prabha, and her spouse Venkatesh, for giving me ideas on the artwork of the cover and the title of the book. I must also acknowledge the contribution of Alyosha's peers and friends for their impressions, which find place in the book. Special thanks are due to his close friends Satyajit Sarna and Arun Srikumar, who may not have assisted actively, but by just being there gave me immense mental comfort. Gratitude to Dev Lahiri, a friend who was also the headmaster at Lawrence School during Alyosha's stay there for writing the Foreword.

Eternal thanks to Shikha Sethi, who painstakingly proofread the text, and without whose efforts the book would not have seen the light of the day. She did this out of her love and regard for Alyosha.

I cannot thank enough, Joseph P. Chacko, the 'sutradhar' of Frontier India Technology for publishing the book even though the subject of the book is no celebrity. He also did this because he was deeply affected by Alyosha's persona.

Finally, I must acknowledge the strength given to me by Alyosha himself, whose presence I feel within me each living moment and whose soul gives me the energy to propel onward in life. He lived a short life but, surely, within that duration 'blazed like a shooting star'.

~ 1 ~

Foreword

If I were to be asked what is the first thing that comes to my mind when I think of Aloysha, my answer would be that Aloysha came to all of us as a blessing. And as is the case with all blessings, whoever sent him made sure that he took him back quickly, lest we lesser mortals start taking the blessing for granted.

And in the short while that we were privileged to have him with us, Aloysha touched all the lives around him very deeply. My earliest and perhaps most vivid memories of him are of a ten year old, sitting opposite me on the sofa in my living room at the Lawrence school in Lovedale, a twinkle in his eyes, but a serious expression on his face, asking some of the most searching questions about the way things were being done (or not done) in school, that I have heard from anyone, leave alone a ten year old. As a relatively young headmaster (without the benefit of the years that I have now), his behavior to me smacked of insolence, and even arrogance. But I do remember distinctly feeling that this boy was a complete misfit in the rough and tumble of a boarding school. He would never last the course, I thought, as he was far too sensitive for the rather harsh and demanding world that his parents had chosen to leave him in.

How wrong Aloysha was to prove me! He had an uncanny ability not to let what must have been very upsetting get to him, and focus in an almost yogic way on the goals that he had set for himself- both in the classroom and outside it. And it was not that he was selfish or insular. On the contrary, there were several occasions when he brought along to me a friend who needed an adult to reach out to him. And in his gently persuasive way, he would urge the friend to pour out his troubles, constantly reassuring him that we would do everything possible to help. I know that because Aloysha was so different, and boarding schools, particularly with strong military traditions are very intolerant of "different", Aloysha was given a very hard time by his peers and seniors. It did not surprise me that many of his friends were his juniors. Yet, in his inimitably stoic way, Aloysha never once complained about any "personal' issues". His complaints, if any were always about systems, and always accompanied by suggestions for improvement.

After I left the Lawrence school, I had the good fortune of staying in touch with Aloysha's parents, and through them, of keeping track of Aloysha's career. His life was cut short so brutally and tragically, but I like to think that we were at least privileged to bask in his somewhat near-mystical presence for at least a while. Not everyone receives such a privilege. And I am sure that memories of him and what he stood for will continue to inspire all those who received that blessing.

After having left school, Aloysha continued to hone his empathy for the less-privileged and for all those who needed to be reached out to. And he did this in his own quiet, unobtrusive way. It is indeed in the fitness of things that his parents launched the Brave New World Foundation, whose whole aim is to keep Aloysha's ideals alive. Trotsky is once supposed to have said," They only die who do not live on in others". Aloysha, particularly through the noble work of this Foundation, continues to live on amongst us and it behoves all of us to keep his wonderful legacy alive and thriving.

Dev Lahiri, Ex- Headmaster at the Lawrence School, Lovedale

Alyosha & his Parents soon after he joined at Lovedale

Introduction

It was a Saturday evening on 29 September 2007, which changed our lives forever. I was watching the musical serial 'Sa Re Ga Ma Pa' on Zee TV in my Moscow apartment. My wife was visiting her youngest sister in Bahrain. She had called me up in the evening around 10 P.M local time to enquire after my well-being. I told her I was watching the above-named serial. She in turn told me 'I'm in paradise', and elaborated that she and her sister, along with a few others, were in a resort in the middle of the desert, which was like being in paradise. We had a brief conversation and hung up.

It was precisely while this conversation was taking place that simultaneously a tragedy of monumental proportions was unfolding in Nagarbhavi, a suburb of Bangalore near the National Law School. A short while later, I got a call from an erstwhile colleague and a dear friend of mine from the Navy, Satyen Shukla, who was in India, informing me in a very distressed voice that

Alyosha, our son, had been stabbed and had been rushed to a Wockhardt hospital in Bangalore. He had been informed of this by his daughter Neha, who had been a senior schoolmate of Alyosha's at The Lawrence School in Lovedale. She herself had been informed by Satyajit Sarna, a roommate of Alyosha's at the Law school. The information was rather sketchy and I immediately called up my senior colleague from the Navy, Cdr Bopaiya, who was also Alyosha's local guardian and broke the news to him. It was nearly midnight in Bangalore, and he told me that he would set out for Nagarbhavi forthwith.

Soon after that call, Neha telephoned me and repeated the news and told me that Satyajit was trying to reach me. Just before hanging up, I heard her sobbing. I tried calling Satyajit a couple of times on the number Neha had given me but received no response. In the meantime, I informed my sister Prabha in Bombay and my sister-in-law in Bahrain of the incident, and implored her not to break the news to my wife as yet. I tried Satyajit again and mercifully was able to get through. He then gave me an account of the incident.

Alyosha and his friends (three boys and two girls) were headed back to the hostel in his Maruti 800 after celebrating his graduation at a restaurant, when his car ran out of gas in a desolate place not far from the Law school in Nagarbhavi. They were in the process of seeking help from passing auto rickshaws to fetch petrol from the nearest filling station. They'd managed to get hold of one and were probably haggling for the fare. As this bargaining was on, a SUV with four people in it approached them and prevented them from hiring the auto. They had observed the girls in the car and sensed an opportunity. An argument ensued with some physical jostling. In the melee, another two ruffians passing on a scooty joined in and one of them tried molesting one of the girls in the car. In the ensuing scuffle, wherein Alyosha tried defending her, he was stabbed and had been rushed to the nearest Wockhardt hospital in a vehicle passing by, which his companions had commandeered. I asked Satyajit if he had suffered a stab over his heart but he was not sure, because he had not been present at the incident spot, but had received him at the hospital and had carried him inside in an unconscious state. When I asked him about Alyosha's condition, he in a faltering and breaking voice said that the diagnosis was 'brought in dead'. It was very brave of him to be able to say it to me, knowing that Alyosha was our only child. I silently admired his courage.

To learn of such a great tragedy would evoke varied reactions, from agonized screams to a physical collapse, but I do not know from where I got the strength to deal with the situation, because I did not react in that manner. I was unusually calm, though I must admit I must have gone into a shock. The uppermost and first thought was to inform all concerned – my brothers and sisters, Cdr Bopaiya (who had just about reached the hospital), my sister-in-law, again imploring her not to break the tragedy to my wife except to say that Alyosha was critically injured and in hospital. I also broke the news to another colleague from the Navy, Cdr Murthy, who was stationed in Moscow as the head of the local office of Larsen & Toubro and had been with us in Vladivostok between 1983–86, where Alyosha was born in December 1984.

The second thought was to ascertain the quickest method of reaching Bangalore. As often happens, when it rains it pours, and the internet in my house decided to take a break, as if in grief, and I had to call up Cdr Murthy and ask him to start looking for tickets. I told him I would be driving down to his house, which was a 20-minute drive from where I lived. He offered to pick me up in a cab, wondering whether I was in a fit state to drive, but I told him that time was of the essence and that I would be fine.

On reaching his house, we did a search on the net and while we were at it, I got a call from my nephew-in-law, who was also visiting my sister-in-law in Bahrain, indicating that I could take an early morning flight from Moscow to Frankfurt, and then take a connecting Lufthansa flight that would arrive in Bangalore just past midnight on the night of 30 Sep/01 Oct. This meant I had just about three hours to get ready and reach Sheremetyevo airport. Having made the decision to take the flight, Murthy and I set out to my apartment, collected my stuff and headed for the airport.

It was very nice of him to accompany me to the airport and oversee the ticketing. He escorted me right up to immigration. It is in times like this that the inherent goodness of human character comes forth, and people strive to reach out with a helping hand. The lady at the ticketing was very helpful and also gave me an invitation to the lounge, gratis. She felt I needed the solitude. Just before bidding adieu, Murthy gave me some very sane advice. He said 'Shed all your tears before reaching Bangalore. Do not cry in front of Deepa, as she will need all your strength.' When I look back after all these years, I could not have received a more sagacious counsel.

I was now all alone, reflecting on the immense tragedy that had befallen my wife and myself in particular and our near-and-dear ones in general. Up to this moment, I had had no time to realize the enormity of the situation. My mind had been single-mindedly focused on what needed to be done. I guess my response could be attributed to my training and experience from the Navy as well as a sub-conscious response to shock. It was only when I was alone in the lounge that the gravity of the tragedy hit me. It brought forth emotions and the natural outpouring of grief. I let the tears run down.

During my journey from Moscow to Bangalore, including a transit halt at Frankfurt for a couple of hours, Alyosha's entire life from his birth in the freezing winter of Vladivostok in December 1984, with all the trials and tribulations his mother went through during his delivery, his early childhood, early schooling, time spent in boarding at The Lawrence School in Lovedale, his homecoming in Vizag and schooling there in the Naval School, our move to New Delhi in 2000, his finishing his Class 12 Board Exams from Modern School, and finally studying at the National Law School in Bangalore went through my mind. I thought of his extraordinary achievements in academics and sports, the various summons before the authorities to answer for his mischiefs, his brilliance in almost everything he did, his impish and disarming smile, his simplicity, but above all his compassion for fellow beings, his kindness and extraordinary intellect and perception of life. Tears kept flowing and I let them till they dried up before I landed at Bangalore in the wee hours of 01 October '07.

Till I deplaned, Alyosha's entire life had flashed through my mind and before my eyes, and in its apogee I came to the conclusion 'This world was not meant for someone as beautiful as you.' This is the line from the famous song 'Vincent' by Don Mclean. The song was an elegy for Vincent Van Gogh whose contemporaries thought of him as weird and crazy, much like many around

Alyosha perceived him. The fact is that such people who don't conform to the set pieces in a society, who are free souls, independent in their thought and actions, are usually termed crazy or mavericks. But in essence these are the people who leave behind a profound message, the meaning of which is understood long after they have gone.

Alyosha had to complete an extra trimester in his final year at Law School. His final exam was on 26 September 2007, in a subject in which the examiner was not too kindly disposed towards him. On 27th, Alyosha called me up in the evening and said 'I have cracked the paper such that the examiner can do sweet f'all to me.' Then he went on to say, 'Today, I feel so relieved and can breathe independence. I am really happy and want to thank you and mamma for having stood by me all these years, despite my iterant irregular behaviour and the troubles that I may have brought upon you. I am truly grateful and count myself blessed.'

I was very surprised at this speech, as it was most unlike and uncharacteristic of him. He was usually monosyllabic and laconic on the phone and for him to speak like that was extraordinary. He also told me that his school friend from Lovedale, Samrat, was coming down for the weekend and that they would in all probability drive down to Gokarna, a pilgrim town with a lovely beach south of Karwar on the

Karnataka coast. I told him that his mother and I had never looked at it that way. In fact, we felt blessed to have him as our offspring as he had mostly done us proud, and the occasional transgressions were only a part of growing up. It was our duty and pleasure to give him the best in education and values and that he had more than lived up to our expectations. I then told him to enjoy and celebrate his success, and for once omitted to mention to him 'Watch your flank.' I do regret that omission.

It was the longest conversation I must have had with him on the telephone in his entire life. Later that evening I wondered if it had any significance, since it was so unusual. Now in hindsight, I am not sure if he had a premonition of what was to come. Maybe he did, if one were to go by an email he sent to his cousin sister (my elder sister's daughter) and her husband with who he had not communicated for years, but chose to do so just a day before the fatal incident. He titled the mail: 'It's been a while sister and wrote: "Dearest Karnika and Jijajee, How are you people doing, in life and work in general? I just had my last exam in college day before yesterday, so I am finished with that. Five rather long and far from painless years of college are over. In some ways, it feels like coming home from a long exile. Now looking forward to working in Bombay, glad to be starting work because I suppose five long years are enough for things to stagnate within one little 20-acre campus. A good lot of my classmates are working there." The rest was the usual stuff.

On a simple reading it appears to be a hopeful expression of beginning a new chapter in life, but the subtext for those who knew him well, may well be saying something else. We will never know. And in any case, does it really matter? He lived a relatively short life of 22 years, 10 months and 20 days. He lived it to the full the way he chose to. He loved and he fought, laughed and cried, was learned yet naïve, excelled in whatever he did, was deeply compassionate and brought laughter to the people around him with his wit and wry sense of humour. Even though the manner in which he went caused immense grief, he was an evolved soul, something that needs to be celebrated and not mourned. This is his story.

~ 3 ~

Birth

Alyosha was a simple, but exceptional, human being. He was gifted with an extraordinary intellect and his IQ exceeded 150. He was born on 10th December 1984 at 15.20 hrs in the afternoon in the far eastern port city of the erstwhile USSR, Vladivostok.

His birth was also exceptional in its circumstances. In what should have been a caesarean section, the doctors chose the conservative delivery and in the prolonged process, Alyosha literally had to force his way out of his mother's womb. He was a big baby and in the delivery process ruptured his mother's pubic Symphysis. Perhaps his tenacity in whatever he did was reflected in the way he was born.

We were 52 Indian families in Vladivostok and about two dozen Indian children were born there. However, due to the circumstances of his birth, Alyosha, unlike other newborns, had to spend the first three months of his life in the maternity hospital with his mother, who had to be treated for her condition. Breastfeeding him was difficult as she was confined to a hammock in the supine position and therefore a special infant feed had to be arranged for him, which in the Soviet days was available only to the more privileged lot. Being a special child, special dispensation was given to him. During those three months, he came to be loved by all the hospital staff, which I am sure contributed to the kind of individual, he turned out to be. He had a sparkle about him and left an indelible impression on whoever he met.

Since breast feeding was a problem, I was given a special permit to draw fresh cow's milk from a Government Dairy in Vladivostok and for which I used to travel daily quite a distance as and when I could scramble time from the hospital visits and my training. It had to be done and was quite an ordeal.

The head nurse in the Maternity hospital, Lyudmila Stepanovna had been assigned the charge of looking after Alyosha. She used to come and bathe him herself and would ensure that all his needs were met. We met her during our visit to Vladivostok in Jun 2014 and it was really a cathartic experience. She was also extremely happy to see us and at the same time sad that the baby she had nurtured had to go in such a manner. She would not take any gift from us but a photograph of Alyosha was enough.

I used to take him for walks in his perambulator in the thick of winter when ambient temperatures used to range from 15-25 below zero. I'm sure this also built into his physique and ability to withstand hardships. His name too was unique. Alyosha is a pet name for Aleksei in Russian, but my family felt it was a good name and Alyosha remained his nom de guerre even in his passport. In his infancy, he hardly ever gave us any trouble. He was a happy child and played in his crib most of the time when he was not sleeping, which was, in the early period, much of the time.

Lyudmilla bathing infant Alyosha

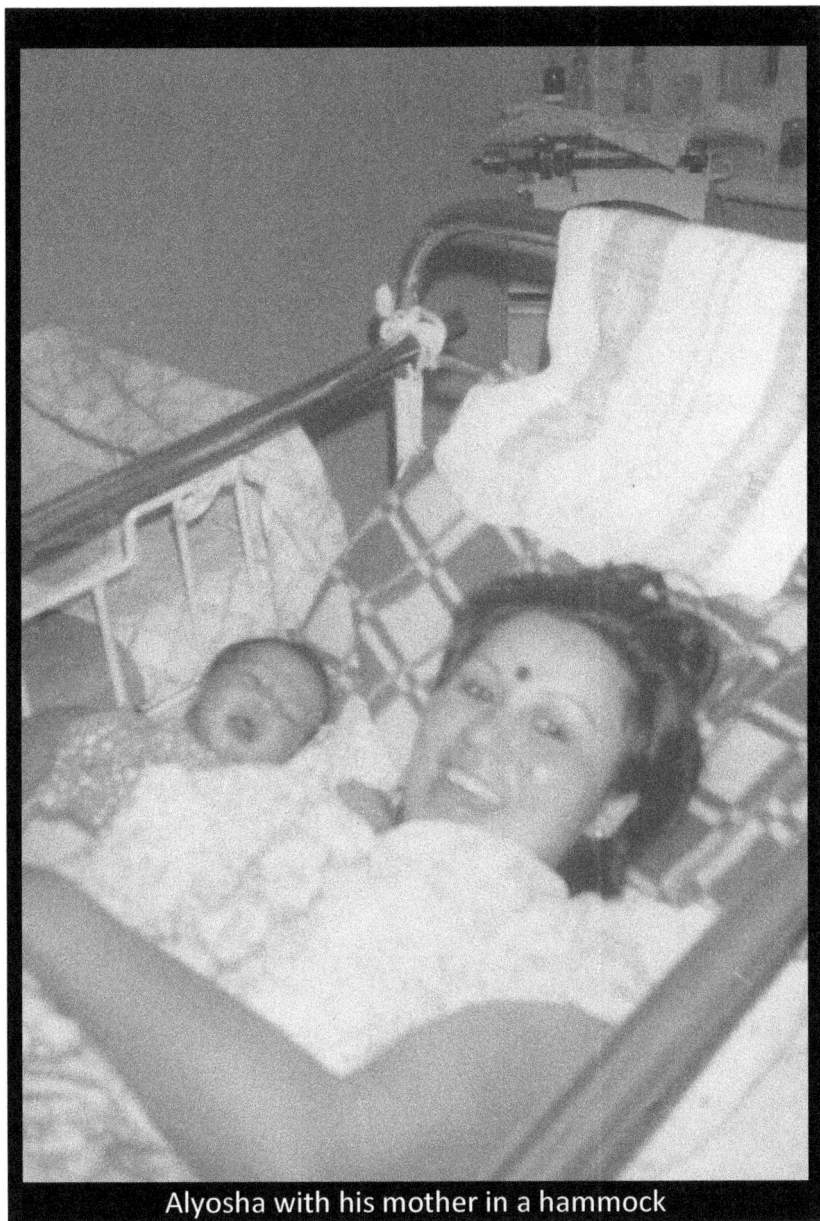
Alyosha with his mother in a hammock

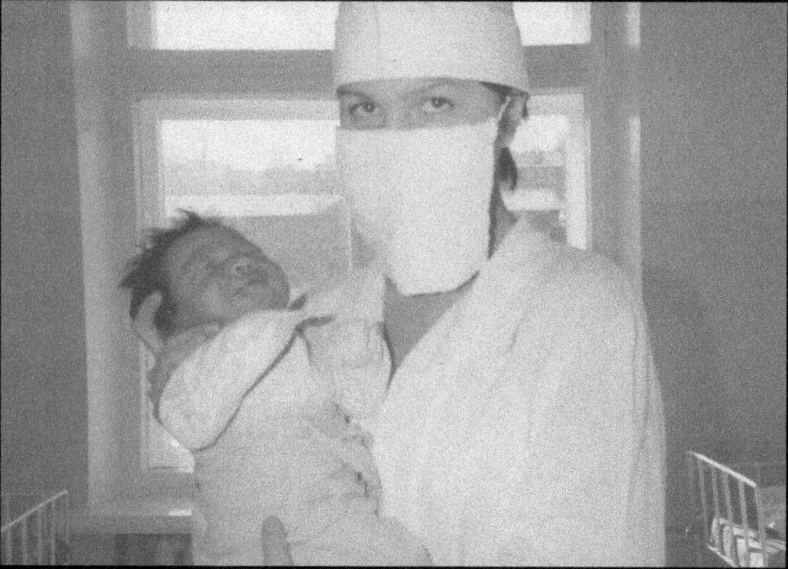

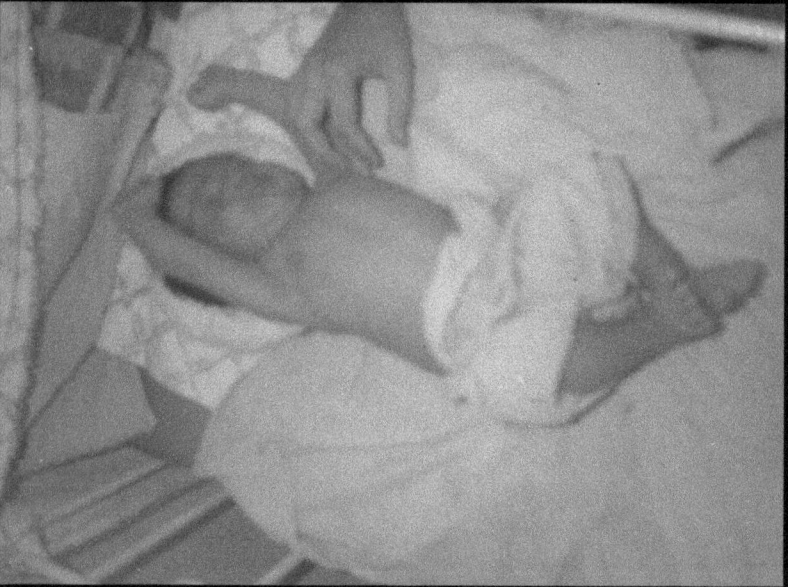

Alyosha with hospital staff

4

The Little Prince

Anyone who has read Antoine de Saint-Exupéry's classic 'The Little Prince' and reflected on it will understand that the story is not so much for children as it is for grownups. Several profound points on human nature and life have been postulated by the author through the personality of the Little Prince (descended on Earth from Asteroid B612), who he saw while hallucinating in the Sahara desert, where his plane had crashed with just a few days' worth of water and provisions. He and his co-pilot were rescued by Bedouins. Exupéry wrote this classic six years after the incident, which had occurred in December 1935.

It is worthwhile recalling some of Exupéry's insights on human life and nature, brought out so beautifully in the story through the Little Prince's interaction with different people in space and during his short sojourn on Planet Earth. The author deals with themes of honesty of purpose and self-centeredness (in the 'Conceited Man'), empathy for others (in 'The Streetlamp Lighter'), commitment and love (the Prince's love for the rose and his commitment to it), inquisitiveness and hunger for knowledge (the Little Prince would never give up on a question, once asked). The necessity to look beyond the obvious as illustrated in the drawing of the boa constrictor swallowing an elephant, which to everyone else looked like a hat and the eradication of ignorance, symbolized in the destruction of the baboa tree (which the sheep must graze on and not let grow).

The need to take time off from one's daily preoccupations to enjoy the beauty of nature as signified in his conversations with the businessman and the railway switch man.

Compassion is the essence of the story, best expressed in the lines uttered by the Fox to the Little Prince: 'It is only with the heart that one can see rightly. What is essential is invisible to the eye'.

Responsibility for one's actions and for what one has tamed is another message articulated by the Fox. 'You become responsible forever, for what you have tamed'.

The other lesson was about the mortality of all living beings. The Prince tells the Pilot that his body resembles an empty shell; he realizes with sadness that the rose he loves so much, is ephemeral, and will wither away one day.

And finally, the book addresses how pretences and outward appearances count for more in our world than actual worth. Remember how the Turkish astronomer's discovery of Asteroid 612 was not accepted the first time by the International Astronomical Congress because of his attire? The very next year it was accepted because the astronomer had dressed up formally.

Alyosha's personality was remarkably like that of the Little Prince. I do not say this only as his father, but as an impartial observer. It was quite obvious to us, his parents, ever since his childhood, that Alyosha was an exceptionally gifted child. His quest for knowledge was not restricted to the classroom. He was a voracious reader and by the age of twelve had finished reading Charles Dickens and Shakespeare. He was presented their complete works by his grandfather, when he was eight.

His taste in literature was varied: He was a great admirer of Dostoevsky, whose classic The Brothers Karamazov was his favourite. He read theology and philosophy whilst at NLS, despite the demanding curriculum. His general knowledge was also truly amazing, and he'd won numerous certificates in quiz competitions as a student.

Alyosha, like the Little Prince, was one who did not accept conventional wisdom at face value. He would always question everything, through the prism of his own intellect and understanding. He was not a nihilist, but his questioning ways did lead him into unpleasant situations with those around him, be it peers, friends or teachers. I reproduce his own words on this aspect. "An incident from the 4th grade still strikes vividly in my memory. It was prep hour and my classmate Celina Stephen was walking hesitantly towards my desk. Seeing her hesitate, I approached her myself. We ended up discussing something in mathematics, but that little exchange broke the back of an ages old institution called 'dame touch' in our school, that had ordained fanatic abstinence from any social or physical contact with the opposite sex. That is one of the earlier stories, in what has been a life of not blindly accepting conventional wisdom, of filtering accepted taboos through the prism of my own understanding".

Alyosha was a simple boy, and had no love for the materialistic world. He would dress simply, as he prided not on outward appearance but on his enlightened mind to make an impression. I distinctly remember that in the spring of 2006, when he went for an interview with a law firm in Mumbai, for an attachment as part of the NLS curriculum, he was simply dressed in trousers and a bush shirt. When asked why he hadn't worn formals, he replied: 'If my clothes are to decide my worth and not my intellect, then I don't think I need to do an attachment here'. The interviewers were not expecting such a forthright reply and post their interaction with him, offered him the position. The following year, the same firm sought him out in the 'campus placement' sessions to work with them on completing his graduation.

Alyosha was an honest boy and in my memory, never ever uttered a lie. In the Lawrence School, Lovedale, in the prep school, he would have become the head boy due to his outstanding all round performance, but did not, because of a small mischief. He sprinkled ink from his pen from behind on the robe of an English Teacher, who had come on an exchange programme from UK. Later he had the courage to own up, knowing fully well that it would cost him the position of the 'Head Boy'.

Alyosha's compassion and empathy for the underprivileged and those in distress was truly remarkable. He had a way with people. In January 2005, when Delhi is at its coldest, he was doing an attachment with an advocate. On one of his trips, he saw the lift man in the building he was staying in, shivering with fever. Alyosha gave the man his jacket not worrying about his own self. When he came home that evening, he bought medicines for him.

After his demise, a prayer meeting was held in NLS after the break in October. During this meeting, a first-year student said a few words on Alyosha. He remembered feeling very intimidated by the atmosphere at the law school when he'd just joined and wanted to leave, till one night Alyosha took him for a walk and encouraged him to fight against the odds and reach his goals. He felt indebted to Alyosha for helping him tide over his insecurity.

During his attachment with the firm in Bombay in the spring of 2006, he helped the security guards in the building his aunt was staying in. I reproduce Alyosha's own account of this narrative. 'About a year ago, I helped secure for the security guards at my aunt's building in Bombay their statutory entitlement to overtime wages, of which they were not aware. The residents of the building were reluctant to make extra contributions towards their monthly subscription, but eventually came around to accepting their basic civic obligations. I felt particularly fulfilled by the fact that my legal knowledge could help those with real legal concerns affecting their everyday life, and that I could help influence the more affluent residents to eventually comply with what is an oft-flouted law'.

But it wasn't just us who saw the Little Prince in Alyosha. There were others too – two people in particular, entirely unknown to each other and from different parts of the globe – who felt the same.

In January 2003, I had sent Alyosha for a short holiday to Singapore. It was a four-night, five-day package. During his stay there, he met a Chinese girl, Li Wenting, studying fine arts. The circumstances of their meeting were extraordinary: Wenting had got locked in her institute, studying late in the night. Eventually, Alyosha spotted her waiting near the fence at the rear gate, not knowing how to get out. Out of compassion, he helped her climb over the fence. They remained in touch over email for two years until he changed his email ID, in 2005, when they lost touch, whilst Wenting kept sending him mail on his old ID, linked to the NLS Server. Two weeks prior to his tragic death, Alyosha, knowing that he would leave the college for good was clearing up his accounts and accessed the server only to see mails from Wenting. They reconnected on email on his new address. They exchanged a few messages, but he could not respond to her final message due to the tragedy of his demise. We accessed his mail, saw Wenting's message and informed her of what had happened.

Wenting was heartbroken; it was over email that she then narrated to us the circumstances of their meeting. She is also an only child to her parents, who live in Shanghai. In the true Chinese tradition of looking after parents in their old age, Wenting adopted us as hers. She subsequently visited us twice in India. On her first visit in May 2008, her primary aim was to give us solace from the grief of having lost our only child, and also to see the place where Alyosha lived.

During her stay, she showed us her pictures of when she had met Alyosha, and I noticed that unlike at present, she was rather on the plump side. I mentioned it to her and then she told us how Alyosha too had remarked to her in his usually candid and forthright manner in January 2003: "Why are you so fat, when all the girls in

Singapore are slim and trim. You look nice anyway." Typical of Alyosha!

On his departure, Wenting went on a weight reduction programme and on being questioned by her friends as to why she was doing it, she replied "because I met an Indian prince, who preferred me to be slim." Her answer took me by surprise. I asked her why she had called him a prince. She replied: "My favourite story is The Little Prince and I saw him in Alyosha." This was in May 2008. I had to tell her then that exactly eleven years back in May 1997, Alyosha had played the role of 'The Little Prince' in a school play during the Founder's Day function at Lawrence School, Lovedale. It could not have been a mere coincidence and to us was really uncanny.

In March 2005, while we were in Dubai, Alyosha had come down for two weeks, during his college break. We visited Al-Ain, a city in the Emirate of Abu Dhabi. Close to that city is the highest mountain in the region known as Jebel Hafeet. We drove up there, to get a view of the landscape and the surrounding desert. There is a plateau on top, where vehicles can also drive up. I still don't know why, but Alyosha went over the fence and stood at the edge of the peak for about five minutes, just looking down at the desert. He would not say why. I later read The Little Prince and came across the passage where the Prince stands on the highest peak in the desert, hoping to see the whole of planet earth, but only sees the desolate and craggy landscape below him, much like the one visible from Jebel Hafeet.

In the winter of 2006, I was stationed in Moscow on business, and Alyosha had come down for New Year's Eve to spend ten days or so with me. We spent New Year's Eve at the 'dacha' (the equivalent of a farmhouse) of a friend. Amidst the merriment, Alyosha made friends with a Russian girl called Mayya'. They hit it off very well, and later she would often visit us in our flat. She also kept in touch with Alyosha via phone and email.

The tragic demise of Alyosha's in September 2007, also hit Mayya very badly and she still thinks of at it as a bad dream, eventually to melt away one day. After the tragedy, it was better for my wife's rehabilitation, (Alyosha was the focus of her life) to move back to Dubai, and my employers were very kind and understanding in enabling the move. In January 2008, I was in the process of packing up our house in Moscow and Mayya was there to help me. Just the day before my departure, she gave me a booklet, printed out from the internet, which she wanted Alyosha's mother to read. She felt that it would help her in coping with the monumental tragedy of Alyosha's loss. I asked Mayya, as to what the printed material was? She said: "It is the story of The Little Prince, I feel reading it will help Deepa." When I asked why this particular story, she said "I saw the Little Prince in Alyosha". I was totally dumb struck. How was it that two girls, unknown to each other and from different parts of this world, saw the same person in Alyosha? I then told her of Alyosha portraying the role of 'The Little Prince' in the school play. She too was taken aback with this strange coincidence.

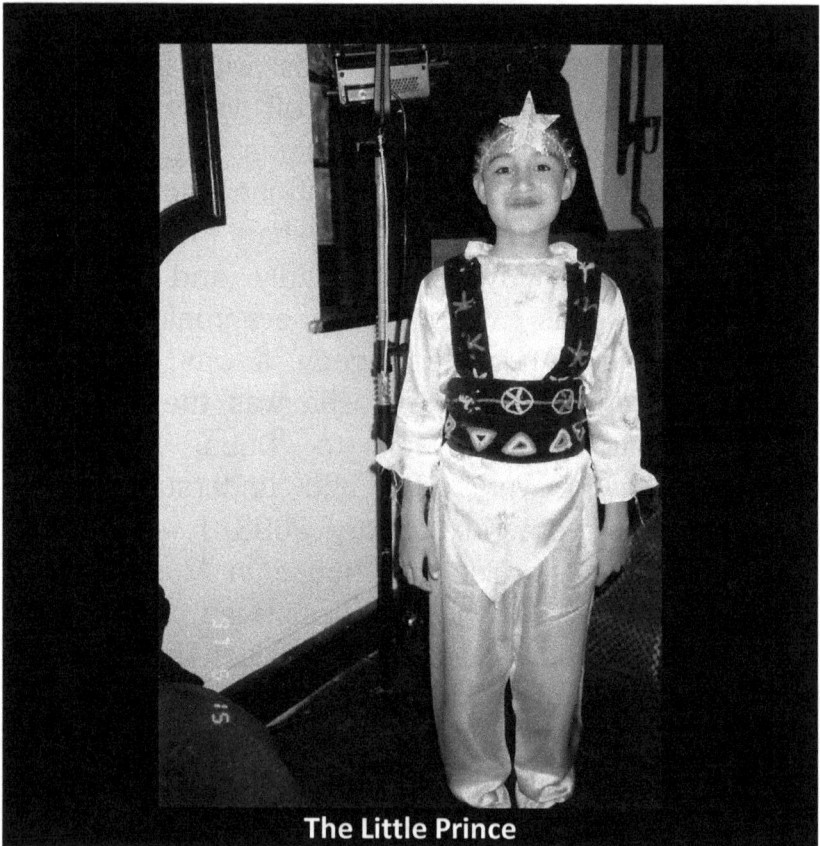

The Little Prince

Like the The Little Prince, Alyosha was a very trusting person. He never imagined that anyone would harm him. In his worldview, there were no inherently evil people. It was his conviction that circumstances made people act the way they did. The Little Prince makes friends with the Snake in the story, and ultimately gets fatally bitten by it. In Alyosha's case too, he was done in by snakes, only in human form.

The loss of our only child Alyosha, is a monumental tragedy, the grief of which can never be totally overcome. It can only be coped with. Each of us comes with his or her own destiny. To quote Paul Coelho, "I am filled by a profound sense of reverence and respect for man who is, at that moment, reminding me of a very important lesson, that each of us have our personal legend to fulfill, and that is all. It doesn't matter if other people support us or criticize us, or ignore us, or put up with us – we are doing it because that is our destiny on this earth, and the fount of all joy". I would add "sorrows" to it.

When Alyosha portrayed the role of the Little Prince in the school play in May 1997, who could have imagined that he was playing out his life? But just as the The Little Prince's message lives on through Exupéry's classic, so does Alyosha's through the charitable foundation set up in his memory, as per his own wish expressed as a nine-year-old boy.

5

The Sportsman

Early days and Football

Alyosha was born nearly flat-footed and knock-kneed. Most infants are knock-kneed at birth, but grow out of it. To be flat-footed and knock-kneed precludes anyone from developing into a good sportsman. However, in these contemporary times, conservative treatments are available to remedy these impairments.

In the initial stages of Alyosha's infancy, we as parents did not do anything as we believed that as he grew up and started walking, the natural growth process would take care of these. In the meanwhile, Alyosha by natural inclination and instincts had a sportsman's makeup. Being half a Gorkha, he had an intrinsic love for football. Also, the 1986 World Cup, when Alyosha was just a year-and-a-half, played its part in channelising his love for the game. Even at that tender age, he would watch the recorded versions of all the world cup matches, (the live transmissions were during the nights, when he was asleep) and wanted to grow up to be Diego Maradona.

Sensing his keenness for football, we encouraged him in every way. He would knock around with a ball just outside the house, as we lived in a ground-floor apartment in Navy Nagar in Mumbai. However, as I have said earlier, his knock knees were a problem. I, his father, had been a footballer of some repute, having captained the team at the National Defence Academy and subsequently being a member of the Navy team. However, I chose to let Alyosha be and not correct him in any manner, because I was convinced that it was not the age to instil any lessons, but for him to just develop his interest in the game and to enjoy himself. So it went on for another year, before we moved to Visakhapatnam in the summer of 1987. Soon after our arrival there – we had not even settled down in our house – when news came of my being deputed to Vladivostok as part of the commissioning crew of the first atomic powered submarine to be leased from USSR. As a result, Alyosha and his mother had to get back to Mumbai, to wait till November 1987, when we were expected to get back with the submarine.

A brief digression here. We spent the next six months starting from Aug 1987 in Vladivostok refreshing our knowledge. We were to take delivery in November 1987, but international political circumstances delayed it to January 1988. It was on 5 January, 1988 that we commissioned INS Chakra, the first atomic powered submarine into the Indian Navy. Our maiden passage back home to Visakhapatnam started on 18 January and after a very eventful passage, including a surfaced transit through the Malacca Straits, we entered Visakhapatnam on 3 February 1988 and were honoured to be received by the then Prime Minister of India, Shri Rajiv Gandhi.

For me, the maiden voyage was even more eventful as we performed an appendicitis operation on a sailor, at 100m depth in the Philippine Sea, in which I became the first assistant to the surgeon on board. I had never seen a man cut up till then, but all the same, it was an experience of a life-time, particularly so as the operation was done under local anesthesia. It lasted nearly four hours, but we had saved a life.

Alyosha, who was then just over 3 yrs and Deepa were there to receive me. It is quite ironic that in those three years, I had seen very little of Alyosha but having got back, I was very happy to notice that his passion for football hadn't abated in the least. In fact, he was even more enthusiastic. Every evening, he would ask me to take him down and play soccer with him. So, it was there in Vizag, that for the first time, he got proper lessons in football. The first and most basic thing to teach anyone in football is that the ball shouldn't be kicked from the toe of the boot, a lesson I had never forgotten since I started in school. This, therefore, was also the first lesson that was taught to Alyosha. Like all toddlers, he was kicking the ball with his toe, 'thudda' as we call it in Hindi, because of the knock-knee problem, which by now had reduced considerably. It was not easy for Alyosha to kick the ball from the inside of his toe, but to his credit and more so because of his consummate passion for the game he was able to do so, and within a month became adept at kicking the soccer ball. Later in his school and college days, he would correct many a colleague on this basic aspect of the game.

Another very important ability for a football player is to be able to use both his feet equally well in kicking the ball. More often than not in younger players, this is the most glaring drawback. When I started off in school, my right foot dominated, but soon enough I was able to develop skills with my left foot too.

The most surprising thing to me was that Alyosha, even at three, was completely at ease using both his feet. It came naturally to him. Later on in his life, I discovered that he was a natural player in most games involving a ball, irrespective of their size, be it cricket, basketball, golf, billiards etc. His telemotor reflexes and the coordination between his limbs whilst playing football was very good and he was very graceful in his play.

As he grew up, his interest in football grew exponentially. He would not miss a single game on TV. By the time he was six, he could rattle off the names of all the top soccer players, which team they represented etc. During his initial schooling at the naval schools in Vizag and in Mumbai, his interest in soccer and his ability with the game made an impression on those around him. He was a part of the naval school junior team in the third standard.

Passion for football unabated

It was around this time in his life when he was 8 years old that we chose to intervene medically to have his knock knee and partial flat footedness, fully corrected. He was given special arched insoles to be put in his shoes, so that the problem would be corrected. He wore these insoles up to the age of twelve, by which time; he had been rid of both and had become an accomplished cross country runner as well.

His passion for football really blossomed in full, during his years at Lawrence School, Lovedale. Both in prep and junior schools, he stood out as a footballer and whenever he had any time to himself, he could be seen knocking the ball around in the Top Flats, where the soccer grounds were located. Whenever he came on vacations from Lovedale, particularly in the soccer season, he would cajole me to take him for Rover's Cup matches in Mumbai. When we were later in Delhi, he would meander off on his own to watch the Durand Cup Football at the Ambedkar Stadium. During his time in Lawrence at the Prep School, Alyosha played for the Vindhya House and was the key member. In fact that would be an understatement, as he was the school's most feared player in the whole of Prep School. His classmate had the following to say of an inter house match:

Niren Mukherjee 1995 – Interhouse football match – Nilgiri vs Vindhya. "Vindhya had the strongest of teams, with Alyosha present, and we (Nilgiri) were not given a second or even third chance. We proved everyone wrong till the dying seconds of the game, when sheer magic from one person won the game for Vindhya. Since all of us were really very short at that time, being the goalkeeper for Nilgiri wasn't an easy task for me. Alyosha made me work my socks off that day. I kept every shot out – all but one. A kick smashed, from close to the half-way line, high into the sky had me back-pedaling and I knew I was in trouble. Sure enough – the ball landed straight in the goal, despite my best efforts. The loss isn't as painful now as it was then but it took a flash of genius from a very talented individual that day to win the game. It was a piece of real class and Alyosha, as always, was his modest self about it. Thank you for that." His understanding of the nuances of the game was remarkable. In his years at the National Law School, his passion for football continued unabated.

During his second year, the college authorities decided to build a library on the soccer ground and I remember how heartbroken Alyosha was. He would tell me: 'These guys in the faculty have no idea how wrong they are'. Land for a library could easily have been found nearby, but taking away an avenue where students could exhaust themselves physically was a recipe for disaster. As it turned out in the ensuing years with no sporting outlets, except for a single basketball court, students drifted into undesirable pastimes.

Kicking the ball as it should be

I remember the summer of 1994 when Alyosha had come down for his first break from Lovedale. We used to live in Mumbai then and were to go to Udaipur to attend my nephew's wedding. The football World Cup was on. Alyosha was not prepared to miss it any cost, wedding or no wedding. He agreed to go with us only after my eldest brother, whose son was getting married, agreed to install a big screen TV in the guesthouse, where we were to stay. Back in 1994, that was a big thing. Even during the 1990 World Cup, when we were in Vizag, he would keep awake at night to watch the matches on television. He was just about six then.

It was not only his passion for playing the game, but also to acquire knowledge of the game's history, its players, about FIFA. He would play FIFA on the desktop for hours on end, when he had time to spare from his literary and academic pursuits.

Although he played as a half-back, he always wanted to take the corners and the direct kicks, as he had learnt the art of bending the ball. Besides, he was a game maker, and had a very good idea of when to use the side, through or the square pass. His favourite team was Brazil and Ronaldinho, his favourite player. Among the clubs, he was an avid fan of Chelsea and Liverpool.

Cricket & Basketball

Alyosha was a natural ball player. Even in cricket, he started early. I remember taking him to watch England playing India at the Wankhade Stadium, in Mumbai in January 1993. When Kambli got his double ton, the joy and thrill the game brought to Alyosha was palpable. Later whilst at Lawrence School, Lovedale, he represented the school's junior team in the Nilgiri's District Schools Cricket, wherein his team won the championship two years in succession.

Here too, his knowledge of the game was phenomenal. Whilst he was at Lovedale, he also picked up basic skills in hockey and basketball.

Somehow, after leaving Lawrence in the summer of 1998, Alyosha's interest in playing cricket waned and he completely focused on soccer and basketball. The latter took less time and virtually no equipment was needed except for a ball and a court. In this respect, Alyosha was fortunate to have facilities available in Lovedale as well as Vizag, because the naval base catered to all the games.

It was thus in soccer and basketball that Alyosha anchored his passion in his final schooling years and throughout his college days. When we moved to New Delhi in April 2000 and were allotted a flat in the Sangli Mess on Copernicus Marg, Alyosha ensured that I got a hard court built for basketball in the premises. I could do so, being the Hony President of the Residents' Association. Help from Military Engineer Service also contributed in the making of the court. It ensured that the officers' children, both boys and girls could get to play without having to travel outside. It saved them time and also reduced their exposure to the hazards of Delhi traffic. Even during his Class 12 Board examinations, he would be seen sweating it out on the court on the eve of every paper, alone, as others were busy with last-minute preparations.

It was at National Law School, in Bangalore that Alyosha chanelled his passion of the game into building a college team, which in the years to come did well in the local and away tournaments.

He was a team man and a physical fitness freak. He would never take the lift in a high-rise building, choosing to run up the stairs instead. A daily run was a must for him followed by thirty to forty pushups. He has described in his own words, how the NLS Basketball Team – particularly of their batch – came about.

Basketball in NLS

He says: "I have also learned with time and experience that when working in a team, it is not always personal plaudits, but the eventual results that matter. In the last three years, preceding December 2006, we have forged a college basketball team from scratch. Being one of the smaller members of the team, the scoring glory goes to the other, taller teammates. I am happy to bask in the glow of victory, knowing I have done my bit – waking up teammates for morning practice, setting an example with my own personal fitness regime while also contributing on court".

Here, his teammate Animesh writes: "I was Al's junior and played with him on our basketball team for four years. He was undoubtedly amongst the best sportsmen Law School has seen, and among the best, I have ever seen. No one could beat Al's tenacity on court, his drive to play hard, with all his heart, no matter what game he was playing. He even managed to win the best hockey player trophy for 2006, and he only started playing the game some two years ago. He was that good.

"Some of the best Law school stories, no, some of the best stories, I have ever heard, have revolved around Alyosha. 'Then when we went for Vellore Baski, this year some three months ago (in 2007), the entire team decided to enter the court together just before the match. On reaching the court, we found Al practising hard, with a borrowed ball, all alone. I could never predict Al and I loved this fact about him.

"Every match we lost against his batch was mainly because he would play out of his skin, every single match we have won as the NLS team was because he was a part of it. He had the patience to teach 'Surd (Satyajit Sarna)' how to play football, one- on- one for so long. Al won the best sports person of 2006 and then proceeded to give one of the most amazing and hilarious speeches, when he was not expected to give one at all."

In fact, Alyosha also won the best sportsperson for 2007. Befittingly, the foundation being run in his memory has instituted an annual 'Gold Medal' for the best sportsperson in National Law School, Bangalore, to be awarded on the annual convocation day. The medal is a full-sized Olympic medal with Alyosha's ever-smiling face embossed on it. It is also gratifying to see that the alumni association has instituted a football tournament, held as part of the sports fest "Spiritus", to commemorate Alyosha's memory.

Golf

Golf was another game that Alyosha took to with great ease being a natural ball player. Golf also being a mind game, Alyosha utilized his intellect very well to understand and play the game.

I had given him a junior set whilst he was in Lawrence School, and he would go to the "Grass Pitch" to practice.

I was then posted in Visakhapatnam. In September 1996, I was deputed to Kochi for 12 weeks for Precommissioning Training (PCT) for command of a guided missile destroyer of the Rajput class. On weekends, I would take a train to Coimbatore and a bus from there on to Lovedale.

On Sunday evenings, I would start back for Kochi and arrive there early morning on Mondays to be on time for my classes.

On one such trip, I took Alyosha for golf to the Wellington Gymkhana Club. It has a very challenging course, laid out in the hills, with tea gardens surrounding it. It offers a picturesque and breathtaking landscape. The fifth hole on the course – a par 3 hole – is extremely difficult. The green is cut out on a sloping hill with hazards and roughs on either side. One has to tee off from about 50m below in elevation and the distance to the flag from the tee is about 170 m. There is a bunker just below the green on the slope.

A good player would need at least a 7 iron to reach the green or the slope above it. Any shank or a hook would mean the ball landing in the jungle to the left/right, with no hope of it being found. If one did not qualify on the green or hit the slope instead, the ball would roll down the hill and set to rest in the rough. Thereon, it would be really difficult to hole out. I have seen very good players take 7 or even 10 strokes on this Par 3 hole to go up and down.

When Alyosha reached the tee, he looked up and said: "Papa, I cannot reach the green, but I would try the bunker". So he set himself up and teed off using his 5 iron of the junior set and landed in the bunker. From there, he chipped on to the green and was up and down in four strokes, thus scoring a bogie. I was impressed by his tactical planning and in playing percentage golf. The first time, to be candid, I thought it to be a fluke. But Alyosha did exactly the same the next day, which convinced me that he had summed up the degree of difficulty and played accordingly.

On the WGC golf course

He did not try to be too ambitious. It showed his scientific and intellectual approach to the game, similar to his manner of tackling any issue or subject.

As long as we remained in Vizag, I would take Alyosha, during his leave from school (usually eight weeks each in summer and the winter) to play golf at the East Point Golf Club. This course too was very challenging. It comprised of fairly rough fairways and browns instead of greens. There were any numbers of palm trees lining up or across the fairways. There were natural rivulets of rain water criss-crossing the course. So one had to be really accurate to stay in the fairways, where one could use a mat or take a preferred lie.

We were in Mumbai for three years from May 92-June 95. The United Services Club in Colaba boasts of a true links course at the southern tip of the backbay. It was here on this course that Alyosha really picked up the game. Things came naturally to him and from the moment he picked up a golf club, his swing developed with ease. I once asked the "golf pro" in the club, Mr Nagraj, to analyze Alyosha's swing and suggest corrective measures. He had one look and told me to leave him alone, as he had a natural swing and that with further development of the body, he would hit the ball real long. This was in the summer of 1993, when Alyosha was just eight-and-a-half years old. In the ensuing months, his aunt Sabena, who lived and worked in Bahrain, got him a junior set. Soon, Alyosha was playing rounds with me at the US Club and learnt the game, as was his wont, fast and well, and was playing to 18 handicap, which at his age was remarkable. He carried this form to Lawrence School, which he joined in the summer of 1994.

In June 1995, I was back in Vizag as the Commodore Submarines COMSUB and in command of the Submarine base there, INS Virbahu. Alyosha had come down for his summer vacations. In the first round at the EPGC, soon after our arrival in Vizag, I took a preferred lie and Alyosha instinctively said "You will muff up your next shot because you have moved the ball." I then explained to him the local rule on preferred lies. However, sure enough, I muffed the next shot, because his words were at the back of my mind.

Golf is a game in which a player plays against the course and his own handicap. No one is watching you, and yet honesty and fair play are essential to become a truly good golfer.

In this respect, Alyosha was fortunate as both honesty and angles in a ball game came naturally to him. I can confidently assert that the true character of a person can easily be gauged on the golf course over one round. It is reflected in how a player faces a situation, be it in a bunker, in a rough or at the apron of the green. The approach and execution reveal his personality. Later, when we had moved to Delhi in 1999 (by which time he had a full set, his junior set having been given away in 1998), Alyosha's ability to give the game time came under stress due to the Board Examinations and once he joined NLS, he was unable to find time for the game. Still, I have no doubt that had destiny not played its cruel hand, in later years Alyosha would have returned to golf and attained professional competence in the game.

A collage of Alyosha's trophies

~ 6 ~

Of Fame and Money

There is a part in each of us that wants to be rich and famous. Rarely does one examine this impulse more deeply.

In January to March 2005, Alyosha was interning in Delhi with an advocate, in the Tis Hazari courts or the lower courts, while his roommate from NLS, and possibly his closest friend Satyajit, was interning with a corporate lawyer practising in Supreme Court. One evening both decided to meet, after work, in the evening and Lodi Gardens was the chosen venue. Alyosha was really fond of Lodi Gardens, as both he and I were regular joggers there with our dog Brutus during our stay in Delhi.

His friend came straight from the corporate office, dressed impeccably, whereas Alyosha was waiting in the lawns in a pair of not-so-clean white pajamas, a yellow T-shirt and a black coat. On his head, he had a Muslim prayer cap, which he had bought from Jama Masjid. They talked about various issues, including how the Supreme Court had majesty over the High Court, even though the avenues for practicing law were more plentiful at the latter. They discussed where one would want to start after graduation. His friend felt that he wouldn't want to struggle for years before being comfortable with the money he would earn. To him, there was no point in waiting and being poor in his twenties. Alyosha retorted that it was not so bad and that there were folks who would pay their juniors Rs 15K a month. His friend almost screamed in frustration at Alyosha's suggestion, when he could easily start at Rs 60K in a corporate law firm. He wanted a swanky office with an AC, a car and all that goes with money and wondered why anyone would want to put themselves through drudgery for fifteen years to get to that stage.

Alyosha sat silently for a while, lit a cigarette and then asked of his friend: "What do want from your life? The money or the fame." Replied his friend. 'Both, ideally. Besides couldn't money buy you the fame?' 'That's not the kind of fame I'm talking about,' said Alyosha. It started to drizzle and both of them went down the street for a drink and the conversation did not continue. But the question lurked in his friend's mind. He did not understand then, that it was a kind of test. He sensed Alyosha did not mean celebrity; he meant fame, which can't be bought. To achieve fame, one has to live a life that makes a difference to those around you in particular, and society at large. Being good or proficient at your vocation does not bring about greatness by itself. What does is, how your proficiency has helped in transforming the lives of those around you. How one has been an inspiration to others? This is what Alyosha was trying to convey. As a father, I exactly know what he meant. He would often say that people need to live their life meaningfully in order to make a difference. The easiest thing is to drift with the tide, but to swim against it and create a new path that changes the status quo for the better is what one should strive for. The fame that comes with such a course of action is real fame. It cannot be bought, it has to be earned.

Material wealth never had much value for Alyosha. He was more engaged in enriching his intellectual wellbeing. Through his growing years, we were rather fortunate that he never made demands for material goods or toys. He was always happy with whatever he got and with what we could afford. We invested in giving him the best education and that really mattered to him. He loved books and would acquire them in numbers. To economise, he would buy the paperback editions from numerous footpath venders. Thrift to him came naturally. He, however, never hesitated to indulge in charity. He would gladly give away to the needy whatever he could, be it in the form of cash, clothes or footwear. He liked to roam barefoot on the roads.

I remember an incident, when one of his

juniors at law school met with a motorbike accident. It was Alyosha who got him admitted to the hospital, and withdrew a large amount from his account to pay the hospital deposit, without batting an eyelid. People would use his car, often without bothering to inform him, but it did not annoy Alyosha. He was generous and large-hearted, a trait he imbibed from his mother. On occasions he would reprimand his mother, if she bought him clothes, which he felt he did not need, but as mothers are, she would be doing it to shower her love on him. We used to visit Lovedale, on the occasion of Founder's Day, every year at Lawrence School. There would be a short break of three days after that, and we would take him out. He always made it a point to bring along those classmates whose parents had not been able to make it. He genuinely felt that he owed it to them. It showed his compassion and understanding of human nature. It's a real pity that his life was cut short in such a tragic manner as he could have made such a difference to those around him. The solace is that even in his short life he touched so many lives. Just the other day, a junior of his from Law School sent me a message: "I might not have known him well, but I will never forget your son. He has been an inspiration to many and my heart aches for you. But it is the world that should weep, because the loss is theirs. All my love, just a junior from Law School."

~ 7 ~

The Egalitarian

Alyosha was a very conscientious person when it came to human relations and dignity. I do not recall a single incident in his life wherein he ever looked down on anyone. He had an intrinsic understanding of human relations. Perhaps his love for animals in general, and dogs in particular, gave him this insight and a sense of fair play when dealing with human beings. Animals do not discriminate on the basis of caste, colour or faith.

When we were living in Delhi between 2000-2004, on my last posting at the Naval Headquarters, we had our living quarters in the Service Officer's Apartments in the old Sangli Mess area on Copernicus Marg. We were in a four-wing, eleven storey apartment block on the tenth floor. There were three elevators in the building. First, a larger one for baggage and the other two for use by passengers. As is usually the practice in defence premises and areas, access to various places is marked, mainly for purposes of efficiency, smooth flow and effectiveness. Accordingly, the lifts in the building had been marked. The baggage one for 'Servants & Families' and the other two were for 'Officers & Families'. I may also mention that each flat had an attached servant's quarter. So the servants and their families had a large inliving population.

I was the honorary President of the residents' association. One day, soon after we had moved into our allotted apartment, which was in July 2000, Alyosha came up to me and said "Who do you think you are?" I was taken aback at this frontal attack and asked him the reason for his aggression. He replied "Why on earth, in the 21st century, are you practising apartheid when it had been abolished even from its last bastion of South Africa way back in 1992?" I did not comprehend what he was alluding to. When asked to be more specific he told me that he was aghast and had taken umbrage at the markings on the elevators, which I have referred to above. I tried to explain to him that in defence establishments, it is customary for such delineations to be made and that the intention was not to segregate.

Alyosha would not buy any of that argument and retorted "Call it what you may, but to me it is pure and simple apartheid. Why can't the servants or members of their families share the lifts with officers and their kin as long as due and common courtesies are observed?" He was fully convinced that this regime of division was not acceptable and that the notices marked on the elevators should be removed/erased forthwith. I realized that no amount of reasoning and references to military customs and discipline was going to change his views. He even reprimanded me by saying "I could never expect you, of all people, to be condescending in such a manner." He told me in no uncertain terms: "Have these markings removed without any delay."

I was in a quandary as this distinctive regime had been in place for years before we had moved in. Also, I was in no position to take a unilateral decision on the issue. However, in my heart I knew that Alyosha was right and had shown us the mirror. I therefore convened a meeting of the executive committee of the residents' association and put the issue before them explaining the circumstances in which the matter had come up. The other members (all officers from the three services of the armed forces) were as taken aback as I had been initially; as each one felt that there was nothing out of the ordinary in so far as defence premises are concerned. However, looking at it from an impartial and neutral perspective, such as that articulated by Alyosha, it did seem unjustified. All of us were compelled to introspect and after some deliberations, I must candidly admit, all the committee members came round to not only accepting Alyosha's view but to endorsing it. My job was made easier in ordering the removal of the demarcation of the elevators.

The above incident also brings forth the issue that the easiest thing to do in life is to flow with the stream, but one is tested when he/she challenges the existing or conventional path. It is only then that the true strength of one's character is exposed. None of us, even senior experienced officers ever gave the issue highlighted above a second thought. We just went along with a practice which had been in vogue for several years. It took the thinking mind of 16-year-old boy to challenge status quo. Alyosha forced us to introspect and made us realize the double standards that we had been following.

There was this lady who sold tea and cigarettes outside the Law School gate and who everyone from the school would call 'Amma' but Alyosha used to call her 'Namma Amma' which in Kannada means my mother. I remember he bought a two-in-one radio-cassette player for her during his visit to Dubai in October 2004, so that she would have something to entertain her in her kiosk. After his passing, we visited the Law School and met her and asked if Alyosha owed her any money as it is usual for students to buy on credit. Her reply was "No, he had cleared all his dues. However, it is not he, but I who owe him so much for all he did for me and for treating me as his own amma." Alyosha would treat everyone he liked as his own. It needs recalling that he was also funding her granddaughter's education out of his pocket allowance.

It was not only the equality of human beings that he was so passionate about. He also deeply respected other people's beliefs. He once asked me "What do you think of gays?" This was sometime in late 2002 or early 2003. I was quite amused to hear such a question from Alyosha. I replied "I do not think anything of them." He was not one to give up so easily and persisted, as he felt my reply was an evasion of the issue. I then suggested to him that if the purpose of sexual intercourse was to procreate as deigned by nature and that since homosexuality didn't fulfil this purpose, such a state was in conflict with the natural order. He saw my point, but was not satisfied. As he saw it, being gay was a physical disposition due to natural instincts and that it was not fair to term it unnatural as I had suggested. I then said that it was a personal view and each one was entitled to have his own. He did not give up and asked "Do you approve or disapprove?" I told him that my previous answer was adequate and that on reflection, he would see its essence. Specifically, I had no particular stand on approval or on disapproval of such a trait in a person. I would gladly interact with one on a purely humanitarian basis. Not fully convinced, he disengaged. However, it got me thinking as to why he had raised the issue. Was there any personal angle at play?

My fears were put to rest when I discussed the issue with his mother the next day. She told me that there was a gay colleague in his class at law school who used to be shunned by the rest of the class. It was Alyosha who empathised with him and accepted him for who he was, and interacted with him as he would with any other individual. This once again gave me a deeper insight into Alyosha's personality. He was not someone who would discriminate against another fellow being just because of his/her station in life or for his personal beliefs. I guess it stemmed from his vast reading of literature and philosophy, which enabled him to understand the complexities of human character. He was perceptive when dealing with individuals and had the ability and wisdom to deal with them with kindness and grace.

He understood human pain, misery and people's aspirations. When he was in the 11th standard, he once told me "Papa there are so many bright children who are socially disadvantaged. They drop out of schools so young due to their inability to cope with the English language. Why can't something be done for them?" I agreed with him completely. Personally, I am a firm believer that primary education must always be imparted in the mother tongue. A child's intelligence and communication skills are best harnessed through the mother tongue. Through my naval career, I have had the good fortune to travel round the world and without exception, I haven't come across any country where the medium of instruction at the primary level was anything but the mother tongue.

The above thought from Alyosha, coming as he did from a privileged background, was an eye-opener for me. I understood that he was not just another child or boy. He was special. He truly believed in equality and was convinced that it was a necessary prerequisite for any society to progress and prosper. Unless equal opportunities at the basic level are provided, no amount of affirmative action, such as reservations, in higher education will deliver any good. As it usually happens, the benefits of such a course of action usually benefit those with vested interests. We see it around us all the time.

~ 8 ~

Random Incidents

In December 1988, I had just finished my SM Commanding Officer's course and had reported back to INS Chakra, the nuclear boat the Indian Navy had taken on lease from the then USSR. I was to leave the submarine the following month to take up my own command of a kilo class submarine. The Chakra was in dry dock. I was going for an evening round of inspection of the boat. Alyosha, who had just completed four years, came along with me, as he wanted to see the submarine from the outside. Access to the Chakra was very strictly controlled, and one had to dress up in special clothes to observe radiation safety regime. On reaching the boat and after having changed into special clothing, I showed him the boat from the dockside. Access inside the submarine was permitted to only the crew and to others by special clearance from the appropriate authorities. I could not have taken him down with me. The duty chief insisted on taking him for a walk around inside and said no one will know. However, I asked him that if he were to go on board, how he would respond to anyone if asked to explain his presence. He replied "I would tell them, I was 'on' and not 'in' the Chakra". I was really taken aback at this reply from a four-year-old boy, who had perfectly understood this nuance of the English language. This was so despite the fact that Deepa and I had endeavored to speak to him only in his mother tongue, Hindi, in his initial years. To date, when I think back to this incident, Alyosha's intellect and quick wit never fails to amaze me.

Another example of his quick wit comes to mind from August 1988, when Alyosha was just three and half years old. We had recently installed an AC in his room at home. One afternoon, I took him along with me to my office. We went in our Premier Padmini, which too was an AC car. Those days only Ambassador and Premier cars were on offer and for a young naval commander, to have an AC car was a bit of a novelty. When we reached my office, which too was air conditioned, a privilege for the crew of INS Chakra, Alyosha remarked in Hindi, "Papa, kamaal kar diya, ghar mein bhi AC, car mein bhi AC, aur office bhi AC". It meant "Papa, you have done wonderfully, AC at home, AC in car and one in the office as well". I really laughed out loud.

As I have said earlier, in the initial years we conversed with Alyosha only in Hindi, unlike many parents who choose to use English, so that his young mind would not get confused. As a result of this, Alyosha's grasp of language and grammar got honed very early and he was never stuck for words. He imbibed English by reading children's comics and classic pocket books.

Yet another instance of his sharp wit comes to my mind. This was sometime in 2006, when Alyosha had finished his fourth year at the National Law School. We were in Delhi, staying with a close colleague from the Navy, who was also a Commodore. He is short in height, standing at 5 feet. We usually referred to him as Napoleon. He was, those days having some legal problems in the Navy, and one evening casually asked Alyosha, "So Aly, will you take up my case, now that you are a lawyer?" Alyosha quipped: "Uncle, I only take clients who are over five feet in height; moreover, you wouldn't be able to afford me".

~ 9 ~

Brutus

alias Mukeshwaran

Alyosha was used to dogs ever since he was a baby in arms. As a six month old, he had stayed with is aunt (mausi), in the summer of 1985, when his mother and he had to come back from Vladivostok, due to the post-natal problems his mother had to undergo. I was still required to be in Vladivostok to complete my training there, which was to end in April 1986.

Alyosha's mausi, (maternal aunt) had a golden Labrador called "Esobbee" endearingly called 'Soby", who was by then already nine years old. For Soby, baby Alyosha was a real object of affection and he used to indulge him in abundance. Alyosha would ride on him, pull his ears, but Soby really loved him, as most Labrador's are wont to do, especially infants.

A couple of years later, Soby passed away and Alyosha was really heartbroken. However, by then we had moved to Vishakhapatnam and

Alyosha's aunt was in Mumbai, so even though Soby had left a lasting mark on Alyosha, somehow he had internalized his grief for him and his love for pet dogs in general.

Alyosha with Soby

Over the next few years, (the initial years of Alyosha's childhood) we moved on posting a couple of times, first to Wellington (Nilgiri Hills) in Jun 1991 and in May 1992 to Mumbai, where we remained for the next three years. During this period Alyosha had already been to three different schools and keeping in mind, the frequency of our transfers in the Navy, we had decided to send Alyosha to a residential school. The choice fell upon the Lawrence School at Lovedale (Ooty), which Alyosha had seen during our stay at Wellington. It was no surprise that Alyosha topped the all India entrance examination for Lawrence School and joined up there in the spring of 1994.

During all those intervening years since Soby's passing away in 1987, I had noticed a yearning in Alyosha to own a pet dog, in particular a Labrador. He, however, never openly said so to me, knowing that I was not much of a dog lover, even though I would tolerate them. Being a single child may have further strengthened Alyosha's desire to have a companion. However, once he had joined Lawrence, this desire of Alyosha's too retreated into the background. But I dare say that somewhere deep within him, it was very much there, though dormant.

During our stay in Mumbai, Alyosha made friends with Aditya, a class fellow in Naval School. Aditya's mother also taught there and both our families became close to each other. Aditya and Alyosha spent most of their free time together and both got along very well on the intellectual plane too. Often they would be at our place or at Aditya's, who had a golden brown Labrador named Brutus. Alyosha grew very fond of the dog and I suspect that later, he named his own pet too by the same name.

After having joined Lawrence school, whenever he came home on vacations, his love for dogs would show as he was always tending to strays and pets among the circle of ours and his friends.

In the summer of 1998, whilst we were posted at Vishakhapatnam and Alyosha had finished nearly half of the academic year in the ninth class at Lovedale, he decided to leave Lawrence and come back home. When I asked him the reason, he quipped "Isn't coming home a good enough reason?" I was literally stumped and had no answer. So was it to be and Alyosha joined up in the Naval School in Vishakhapatnam, from where he completed his 10th Boards in March 2000, aggregating 92%. His scores in Hindi dampened his aggregate, as in all the other subjects he had an aggregate of 94%.

I had moved on posting to Delhi in May 1999, but Alyosha, who had just moved to the 10th, had to stay back with his mother in Vishakhapatnam, as it did not make sense to change school in a Board year. Whilst I was in Delhi, Alyosha's dormant desire to own a pet came to life. He would pester his mother to get him a pup, that too a Labrador. I resisted for a while, as I knew that in a couple years Alyosha would go away to a college and my wife and me, getting on in years, would be left to tend to the pet. In the end Alyosha's persistence prevailed and in early January 2000, we picked a golden brown Labrador pup.

In fact as is usual, in such cases, the pup picked us up. My wife and Alyosha were in

Vishakhapatnam and a colleague friend of ours had a litter of five pups. His son was Alyosha's friend from when we had been in Mumbai last in the early 90's. So when he informed Alyosha about the litter, both mother and son went to pick up a pup. When they fetched up there, the two healthiest ones had already been taken. Out of the three left, the weakest and probably the laziest came and sat in Deepa's lap and the rest is history! Alyosha named the pup "Brutus". I guess this was to honour his memories and fondness of "the Brutus" he had played with in Aditya's house in Mumbai in 1992-95. That dog was also a brown Labrador and an extremely friendly one at that. So the saga of Brutus in our lives began. I was in Delhi at that time and the first time I saw Brutus was when I visited Vishakhapatnam for my annual leave in December 1999/Jan 2000. Brutus was a really a lovable pup and would seek warmth and love from whoever he met. He was a quick learner and responded very well to his toilet training. As it used to be quite warm in Vishakhapatnam, and Labrador's being averse to heat, Brutus would lie on the bathroom floor or in the kitchen next to the drain pipe, so as to keep cool. He was really scared of loud noises such as fire crackers and even exhaust noise of jet aircrafts. He would start shivering and try to find a hiding place under the bed or behind a wardrobe. This fear of his persists to this day and we feel really sorry during Diwali and wedding celebrations when firecrackers are the order of the day. As a larger issue, this is something that we as humans must think over, as not only dogs, most animals get really scared of firecrackers.

Brutus

Would it not be better of us to tone down our propensity to light crackers at the easiest of excuses? In my personal view, it is not only for organizations such as PETA, SPCA but for human beings, as a whole, to really and seriously look at this issue so as to harmonize our coexistence with the animal world, which is so very necessary for ecological balance.

With Brutus as a pup

Coming back to Alyosha and Brutus. With the advent of Brutus, at long last, Alyosha had found a companion at home to communicate and interact with. As parents we can and could never be in that position. He would talk to Brutus all kinds of things, make him sleep with him, fondle his ears in particular and always showed real concern for him. All this, of course, is natural and not uncommon, as most pet owners in general and dog lovers in particular do care for their pets. However, what was exceptional in Alyosha's case and Brutus, was that after naming him Brutus, Alyosha never again called him by that name. Instead he would call him "Mukeshwaran". I used to wonder why, but never got an answer from Alyosha during his lifetime.

As Brutus grew into a handsome dog, the affinity and closeness between Alyosha and him grew in geometric proportions. Alyosha would take Brutus along with him everywhere, except to school (which was not possible), and be it playing basketball in the evening or for walks to Lodhi Gardens in New Delhi. The two were like inseparable souls, who had some preordained divine connection.

In April 2000, we shifted house from Vishakhapatnam to New Delhi and had to travel by train. The journey from Vishakhapatnam to New Delhi was via Hyderabad, where we took a two days break to see some of the historic sites as also the famous Ramoji film city.

We stayed at the Naval Mess in Hyderabad. The vice president of the mess, who I knew, told me that we could not keep Brutus with us in the family suite, which we had been allotted, as it was not permitted. I explained to him that Brutus had been toilet trained and that there would be no soiling of the room and that Brutus was just three months old and would need attention in the night. But the VPMC would not budge. Alyosha then volunteered to sleep with Brutus on the floor of the common toilets. Having overheard all of this, the duty steward came to me later and said "Sir, please keep the pet with you in the suite. I won't let it be known to anyone". I guess he was touched by the affinity and closeness between Alyosha and Brutus.

Travelling in the train with Brutus was not a problem, as the Indian Railway permits pet dogs in AC 1 class, if the dog is properly harnessed. The only issue was that the Rajdhani Express from Secunderabad to Delhi had only one stop, so we had to take Brutus to the WC's in the compartment, in the moving train. Amid all the noise, it was an evolution to get Brutus to do his job. Even in all this, it was Alyosha's coaxing and cajoling, which helped Brutus overcome his fears in the moving train.

After having moved house to Delhi, we were initially staying in an outhouse suite in the naval mess at Kota House. Alyosha was on school holidays, awaiting his 10th Board results. Alyosha and I would take Brutus for an early morning walk to the Lodhi Gardens which were nearby. We made friends with so many other dog owners there and each weekend there would be a dog's get together, where the canines would be given a feast, play football and have a ball! I can vividly see the joy on Alyosha's face on these occasions.

An incident during the early part of our stay in Delhi is worth mentioning. On a weekend in May 2000, we had gone to visit close friends at Panipat. They had a huge, very aggressive and not very friendly, Irish Pointer. When we reached there, he made his dislike for Brutus very apparent and for the next two days, the hosts and we had to exercise great care to keep him away from Brutus, who was still only six months old. However on the day of our departure, we let our guard down a bit, and while we were loading the baggage in the car, The Irish Pointer, appeared from nowhere and came charging and snarling at Brutus, with intentions very clear. All of us stood frozen, not knowing how to react. However, Alyosha keeping his cool simply picked up Brutus close to his chest, rather to his heart. Very surprisingly, all of a sudden, the aggression and hostility of the Irish Pointer subsided and he simply scampered away whimpering. To date, I wonder if the affinity and closeness between Alyosha and Brutus had the force of divinity, which tamed the ferocity of the other dog.

After Alyosha had joined the NLSIU at Bangalore, Brutus was left without a soul mate. He would look forward to Alyosha's visit on vacation after each trimester. The welcome that Alyosha would get on arrival was a treat to see with Brutus clambering all over him. I guess the five years away from home without Brutus, had also affected Alyosha. He was really looking forward to taking residence in Mumbai in October 2007, alongside Brutus after joining the Law firm which had hired him. Most tragically, it was not to be.

In May 2004, I had taken premature retirement from the Navy and taken up a job in the Middle East. However, we kept a running house in Pune so that Alyosha could come home every three months and spend time with "Mukeshwaran". Here I must bring out the role played by Ganesh, our domestic help, who has been with us ever since our times in New Delhi. When we moved to Pune in 2004, Ganesh could have easily stayed back as he hails from Garwhal in Uttaranchal. However, he too had got attached to Brutus and opted to be his keeper in Pune and ever since, he has looked after Brutus faithfully and given him love, care and affection that anyone of us would envy.

After Alyosha's tragic demise, Ganesh has twice decided to go back to his native place, but each time the affinity and his feeling for both, Alyosha and Brutus has brought him back. Strange indeed are the ways of destiny.

When rituals for Alyosha's demise were being performed, and our house was full of relatives, Brutus conducted himself in a really stoic manner. I am sure he had reckoned what had occurred. Dogs have an innate sense with these things. Not once during this period, with all the people around, did he create any fuss or ruckus. To my mind, he too was mourning his soul mate. Just after the rituals, my wife was lying on the bed one night and Brutus was in his sleeping basket, next to the bed. All of a sudden, Brutus put out his front right leg around my wife's neck and (she swears) actually sobbed.

I said earlier, that I often wondered why Alyosha after naming "Brutus" never called him by this name, instead choosing to call him "Mukeshwaran". I tried finding out after Alyosha's demise from a psychic medium and she told me that Alyosha saw divinity in Brutus and related to him spiritually. I really do not know if that is the truth but what we did discover, was that Alyosha had a natural mark of "Vishnu" on his forehead. This can be seen in the picture on the front cover of the book as also in his pic in the chapter "Spiritual Soul II. "Mukeshwaran" is also one of the many names of "Vishnu". To our surprise, in a photograph of Brutus taken on his 9th birthday, in November 2008, the letter 'M' on his forehead was clearly discernible.

The Letter 'M' on the forehead

The same, if turned clockwise, also resembles the Vedic symbol of "OM". I found this rather extraordinary. I consider myself to be a rational person, though not an agnostic or an atheist. But even to me, are these observations mere coincidences or do they have a deeper meaning?

I really cannot say. In a way, however, Alyosha calling Brutus "Mukeshwaran", seems to have unravelled itself. It is for the reader to draw any conclusions otherwise.

~ 10 ~

AU REVOIR

BRUTUS

At 04.20h in the morning of 11th Dec 12 our beloved pet Brutus, alias Mukeshwaran left us to join his soul mate Alyosha in the other world. He lived to the royal age of 13 years and 10 days, which for a Labrador is really a grand old age. For about three months prior to his demise, he had not been too well. He had got paralyzed on his left side and also had developed tumors in his stomach. Given his age, there was not much that could be done, except to manage these ailments, which we, especially my wife, her sister Sabena and the two male helps, did.

Often we got the advice to do what usually is done in such circumstances, but we were prepared to do all that was required to make Brutus as comfortable as was possible and refused to put him to sleep. He was a legacy to us from Alyosha and also that; mentally he was fully alert and displayed the same affection as he had done all his years.

It was difficult to manage, but manage we did. He would indicate when he wanted to be excused and had to be carried. A makeshift toilet had been made in our balcony for him to do his ablutions. It is to his credit that even till the last day, when he did eventually go, he never soiled the house. He was a very civil dog. Even in his usual walks, he would never do his big job in the open or on the path/road. He would always go into a bush/shrub to do it.

His 13th birthday which was on 30th Nov 2012 was celebrated with a aplomb and he fully understood the occasion and found some reserve of strength to move his limbs. May be the adrenalin due to the excitement facilitated this, but it was indeed welcome.

Ever since Alyosha tragic demise in Sep 2007; Brutus had been a great source of solace to us. Without words, he would convey to us that not only he shared our grief, but also that life had to carry on and that we had to cope just as he was doing. Each year at the prayer ceremony on the occasion of Alyosha's death anniversary, Brutus would watch all the preparations sitting close by in stoic silence, but fully alert to the goings on. During the prayers he would sit just behind me and my wife and listen to the entire chanting of hymns and mantras and at the end of it, would retreat to his room under Alyosha's portrait. It was his way remembering and paying tribute.

Towards the end of 2009, Brutus had developed an enlarged heart and therefore we could not shift him to Dubai to be with us. However, we had our apartment in Pune, kept running purely for his sake. We had the old faithful Ganesh to look after him and a year later, his cousin also agreed to be there, so that both could share the work as also be company to each other.

Between my wife and me, we would make a trip every six weeks or so to Pune to spend some time with Brutus. At other times, my sister in law Sabena, who is in Mumbai, would go across to Pune and keep Brutus company. My wife's sister and niece who live nearby in Pune would also visit him often. As a result Brutus always had company and someone to take care of him. He remained his cheerful, affectionate and loving self throughout despite the slowing down of his heart. He would be driven down to Empress Gardens every morning for a walk and had endeared himself to all the watchmen there. The stray dogs there had also got friendly with him.

Brutus had a regal way of walking with his handsome face held high. Any stray barking at him would be ignored royally. It was a real pleasure seeing him conduct himself in that manner. He was also really fortunate in that he was looked after really well. His coat was groomed and powdered daily, as a consequence of which, he never left the typical dog smell in the house. His feet were washed after every walk (which was four times a day) so that he remained tics and insect free. I guess all this attention lavished upon him played a major part in his approach to others. He was a really friendly creature, (Labradors usually are) and would endear himself to anyone who came to visit us.

Dogs are known to have a sixth sense more than other creatures. In my experience with Brutus, this belief was confirmed. I fast on Tuesdays and have been doing so for more than 30 years. Basically I do so, not so much for religious reasons, but for reasons of health, to give the internal systems a rest. I also take the opportunity to visit a temple in the evening before breaking my fast. So, when we were living in Delhi, on Copernicus Marg , I would drive down to Khan Market with Brutus and park my car at the Northern end of the market, opposite a sweet shop (which closed down a few years ago) and walk down to the temple barely 100 mts away. Brutus would remain in the car. On my return, I would give the 'Prasad', which he really relished. I would help myself to 'Paani Puri' at the sweet shop before driving back home. The sweet shop owner always gave me a couple of 'Papris' to feed Brutus. This routine, every Tuesday, had been internalized by Brutus. Whenever I was around, he would, on a Tuesday in the evening, urge me, in his usual manner of a gentle bark, to make that trip to the temple. He would sense the day, by observing me fast.

After my retirement in 2004, we had moved to Pune. There, too I used to visit the Hanuman temple on the Main Street and when I got home, without any prompting, Brutus would come and demand to be fed with the 'Prasad'. It is said that dogs are creatures of habit and I saw this fully endorsed in Brutus' behavior.

Even in Delhi, when we would go for our morning run to Lodhi Gardens, Brutus had shown this facet. I would rise at 0600h (be it winters or summers) and after a wash, meditate for about twenty minutes. During this short time, our friend would remain silent lying in his basket bed, but no sooner would I finish, he would bark ever so gently indicating to me that it was time to go. This sixth sense and also his awareness of the occasion was displayed in real measure just before his death. As I have said that he was paralyzed for nearly two months and had to be carried from one place to the other. Besides, his heart and the tumors in his stomach were also not helping. He could have gone anytime between November and December 2012, earlier than he eventually did. However, he waited for his 13th birthday on 30th Nov 12 to be over and also held on till 10th Dec had passed which is Alyosha's birthday. I remember talking to my sister in Mumbai from Dubai in the third week of Nov, and expressing my concern and apprehension of Brutus giving up at any time. My sister categorically told me, "You just see that he will wait for the 10th of Dec to pass and only then will he go". Prophetic words that actually came true.

On the 10th of Dec, he was really unwell and had been on IV drop for two days. The vet examined him in the evening and said that his end was near. My wife brought a cake and we cut it in front of Brutus to remember Alyosha on his birthday, a practice we had never followed in Alyosha's lifetime. We would celebrate his birthday either a day earlier or later, due to an ominous belief in our family as a member had died on his own birthday. Brutus understood and recognized that it was Alyosha's birthday and despite two really bad alarms, once in the evening and the other just after midnight held on till after 4am on the 11th, by which time, the next day starts as per our Hindu custom. He did not want to go on the 10th Dec and made sure of that, so that we could always remember Alyosha on that day without recalling the grief of Brutus at the same time. To all of us, it was really uncanny.

He went peacefully and blessed us all, who were beside him at that time. He suddenly got enough strength to raise his head and survey us from left to right and then gently put his head down on the pillow and went into eternal sleep. It was really amazing, the manner he had looked at us all, before breathing his last. He looked so peaceful in his final sleep.

We cremated him the same afternoon (11th Dec) in an animal farm at the outskirts of Pune, where such facilities exist. My wife had decided that she will take his ashes to Hardwar for immersion in the Ganges, at the same spot as the one where we had done for Alyosha. Both she & I, eventually did go to Hardwar on the 21st of Dec and completed that last ritual as we had set out to do. Brutus, nay-Mukeshwaran had left on his final journey, to be with his soul mate Alyosha. I am sure they are re-united in the heavens up there.

Au revoir Brutus, you like Alyosha, were a blessing bestowed upon us and thank you for all the love and joy that you brought into our lives.

~ 11 ~

The Spiritual Soul - I

Childhood

Alyosha was a deeply spiritual soul. He had a normal childhood, yet his extraordinary intellect and compassionate nature marked him out as different from his peers. He also had his failings as anyone his age would have. However, it's quite amazing that he was fully aware of his higher nature and had the insight and clarity to understand it at a very young age. I will come back to this later.

He also, somehow, believed in the reincarnation of souls. In his early childhood, even before the age of ten, he seemed fascinated by movies like Araadhana and Karz, which dealt with the theme of reincarnation. These movies were super hits well before he was born.

He would watch these films on the VCR at home many a time in his free time, when not playing games or otherwise engaged. It was fascinating to see him identify himself with the main protagonists in these films. From where this affinity sprang in such a young boy was difficult to fathom. It had to be an inner voice, a spontaneous instinct. I also vividly recall a train journey from Mumbai to Pune in 1993, during which a roaming book vendor walked through our coach. Alyosha, who was about nine then, chose a booklet Reincarnation of Souls from amongst all the books the vendor had on offer. Even later, in his college days, apart from the books relating to his syllabi, he was deeply interested in reading books on theology, philosophy, and literature dealing with the evolution of human life.

This we noticed also from the collection of books that was returned to us in his baggage after his demise. The first book that popped out was 'The Philosophy of Life and Death' by MV Kamath. His favourite author was Fyodor Dostoevsky and his favourite book The Brothers Karamazov. It may not be coincidental that the main protagonist in the book was also Alyosha and a spiritual person. Here, a distinction must be made between religious and spiritual. I would not have termed Alyosha as deeply religious. He was a rational and a questioning individual. However, he was also an innately spiritual person. He believed in the goodness of the human character. He often told me that inherently no person is evil. It is usually the circumstances that drive a person to behave badly. Even on that fateful night of 29th/30th September 2007, when Alyosha met his end, he would never have imagined that someone would try and harm him. Harm him for what? For standing up to molestation, for upholding decency? I understand that the autorickshaw driver had warned him that the hoodlums were armed with knives. Alyosha's typical response was "So what! What can they do to me?"

I also remember an incident in 2003. Alyosha had been home for his first trimester break from NLS and was due to fly back the next day. He asked his mother to put some money in his wallet, so that he could find his way from the Bangalore airport (those days it was operated by HAL) to the NLS campus at Nagarbhavi. So, she put a Rs 500/- note in his wallet. One of his friends came to see him, but Alyosha had gone out to run an errand. His mother told the friend that Alyosha was out. He replied saying, "No worries, aunty, I will sit on the computer in his room till he gets back". Since he lived in the same complex as ours, this was not unusual.

After a while, he suddenly left, without meeting Alyosha. When Alyosha came back and was getting his stuff ready for the next day's journey, he accosted his mother, "I had told you to put some money in my wallet, but you forgot as usual". She then told him that she had indeed put a Rs. 500 note in his wallet, and that during his absence his friend had come so it was most likely that he had flicked the money. Alyosha calmed down and said "No Mamma, he has not stolen it, but has borrowed it and will return it when he can". This little incident showed his intrinsic belief in the goodness of human beings. This brings to mind the story of "The Bishop and the Candlesticks" which most of us read in our school days. Only a spiritual person would have had this approach.

There are several other such episodes and indications after his death that reinforce my belief that Alyosha was indeed an evolved soul with a spark of divinity.

The funeral

On the day of his funeral, 1 October 2007, which was a Monday, it was bright and sunny in Bangalore. I had fetched up there from Moscow early in the morning, as had my wife. After all the formalities of the post mortem, recording of our statements etc, had been completed, we took his body from the mortuary to the crematorium. On the way my wife and I, despite the shock we were in, studied his face closely. He had grown a beard and his facial expression was absolutely calm and serene and he had that impish smile. His eyes, although shut, looked as if they were sparkling as they always did. For us, this was most unexpected considering the brutal end that he had met. It was as if he was telling us, "Don't grieve for me, I have gone in peace". It may sound a bit odd to anyone, but to me his face looked as saintly as that of Jesus Christ, even in the moment of the brutal agony he had suffered.

At the crematorium, we were surprised to

see the number of people who had come to condole with us as well as to bid farewell to Alyosha. The number easily exceeded six hundred. Friends, who we had not been in touch with for years, had turned up. His friends from outstation, including one from London had made it. That he had been such an endearing soul struck us that afternoon. Coming back to the main theme of how bright and sunny the day was. There was no likelihood of rain, even though Bangalore is rather unpredictable in this regard. No sooner had his cortege rolled into the furnace; it started pouring as if the heavens had burst. The heavy downpour lasted just twenty minutes, the duration of the cremation in the furnace, and stopped as suddenly as it had started and the sun shone again. But in those twenty minutes, the compound of the crematorium got flooded up to our ankles. I remember my sister saying that Alyosha had found salvation and what had just occurred was a sign of that.

To a rationalist, and I count myself as one, this may sound far-fetched, but what explains such an occurrence? It was not an ordinary, usual downpour. It was as if the heavens were also shedding tears at the loss of such a pure soul. Of course souls never die, they only change states.

The Narayan Bali ritual

In the mid-October 2007, we had to go to Varanasi to perform a ritual called 'Narayan Bali', which is usually performed by Hindus, in the event of an untimely death of person before he/she had attained the age of 25 years. We travelled by road from Lucknow to Varanasi. It was the period of 'Navratras', the festival of nine nights of prayers and abstinence from meat, in worship of the Goddess Durga. After nine days, the deity is taken for immersion accompanied by pomp and glory. This is the usual practice in Northern India and Bengal, but on the highway from Lucknow to Varanasi, one has to pass through Sultanpur District, where instead of nine days, the festivities go on for nearly two weeks.

Although we had travelled after the designated nine days, we ran into processions on the highway in this district. The road was blocked and no traffic could proceed. We were redirected to use the bylanes of the villages in that district, including driving through fields. It was already after sunset and it was dark. With no lights to illuminate the so-called roads/by lanes, it was a nightmare to drive. For even here, the narrow bylanes were taken up by people taking their deities for immersion. My brother-in-law was driving (my wife's elder sister's husband). He had to be careful while manouevering the car, because if it had touched even one person, we could have faced the wrath of the mobs that thronged these bylanes.

It was crawling through such crowds that we somehow managed and got back on to the highway after about three hours. We still had a two-hour drive to Varanasi. Incidentally, these villages in Sultanpur District, which fall in the 'Amethi' Parliamentary Constituency, are represented by none other than Mr Rahul Gandhi, had no electricity. They were making do with petromax lamps. I found it rather strange that even 60 years after Independence, the constituency of the scion of the first family, was in this state of development, or rather the lack of it.

We had been on tenterhooks throughout the drive, and finally reached Varanasi past midnight after a seven-hour journey, which normally should have only taken four hours. Exhausted, we all fell asleep as soon as we hit the bed. Next morning whilst having breakfast, we saw on the TV that there had been mini riots precisely in the area that we had traversed through the previous evening and that there had been, if I remember correctly, two deaths as a result of police firing in trying to control the mobs. All four of us – me, my wife, her sister and her husband, were struck by the fact that we could have got embroiled in those riots with god knows what consequences. We counted our blessings for having come out unscathed. It was then that we reflected and felt that it was the soul of Alyosha guiding us to our eventual destination safely. It may sound irrational or coincidental, but all four of us had the same feeling.

In September 2008, we observed the first death anniversary of Alyosha at our home in Pune. There is the usual prayer invoking peace to the departed soul, followed by lunch for twelve priests, close relatives and dear friends. As per the Hindu calendar the date fell on 20 September. Prior to that, it had been raining incessantly for three days with no respite in the offing. We were anxious as to how the havan, which formed an essential part of the ritual, would be conducted. On the morning of D-Day, the rains stopped. The sun came out. The entire shradh ritual was conducted without hitch. We finished by about 3pm in the afternoon. No sooner had everything been secured, the skies opened up once again and it rained for the next day and a half. It was as if the Lord Indra (the rain god) had been kind to us to facilitate the completion of the ritual as planned. Or was it Alyosha's soul that had intervened to ensure that all went as it should have?

Setting up The Brave New World Foundation

We have set up a Public Charitable Trust in Alyosha's memory, as per his own wish. Now in India, to start anything one has to deal with the bureaucracy, which is not simple. There are rules and procedures, but even if one has meticulously followed all of them, nothing will move forward unless the decision makers are paid illegal gratification.

Initially we faced many problems at the Charity Commissioner's office. It was obvious that many questions were being asked about the Trust Deed just to make things difficult. However, finally, with the help of some of my contacts and also facilitation by Alyosha's spirit, the trust was registered without any hitch in June 2008. The next step was to get an income tax exemption for the income and donation that would accrue to the Foundation.

The application to the Director, IT (exemptions) was submitted in early July 2008. One day in mid-July, I was in Mumbai and decided to call on him to personally to explain the motivation for setting up the Foundation. It was around 10.30am when I reached his office in Parel. For a Central Government office, it was still early for work to start and there was a notice outside his office, which stated that personal meetings were only permitted in the afternoon between 1500 – 1600h. I had, however, only the forenoon at my disposal and decided to knock and go in.

The gentleman was actually dusting his chair and desk and surprised that I had just walked in. He even said to me, "Did you not read the notice outside my office?" and "How come my staff let you in?" I replied that no one was present outside and I had taken the liberty to walk in, as I had only an hour, and was to leave the city to go abroad that very afternoon. I introduced myself and he was gracious enough to attend to a retired Commodore from the Indian Navy.

I explained the purpose of my visit and requested him to expeditiously process our application for IT exemption, which we had submitted only a few days ago. I also wanted to apprise him of the reason for which the trust had been set up. After explaining the circumstances surrounding Alyosha's tragic demise, I asked him to read Alyosha's 'will' of sorts. The same written in Alyosha's own hand at the tender age of nine and half years. It is at the beginning of the book as a curtain raiser and needs to be read as written. On reading the same, Mr Sinha, the Director IT (exemptions) was touched and said to me, "Your son was a gifted child." Although I knew it, I asked him why he thought so? He replied, "No child of that age can ever think of such a profound thing, leave alone putting it to paper in such lucid and unambiguous language. Dare I say, even grown-ups would find it difficult to write like that." He then told me that the minimum time for processing the application was three months and that could not be reduced, but he assured me that three months from the date of application, his office would call us to get the needful done. He also advised me to keep all the documentation, book of account etc updated for inspection at the next meeting.

True to his word, on exactly the 90th day, he invited my sister, who is a Holding Trustee in the trust, to his office. His immediate deputy, a lady, was to conduct the meeting. Before she had even started, she insisted that first she would like to read Alyosha's will. Obviously, it was the purity of his soul that had permeated in that office. After she had verified all the documents, ledgers etc, she approved of the exemption and also said to my sister: "You must do all that is necessary to fulfill Alyosha's wish, as extremely rarely does one come across such a vision from a mere boy". When my sister conveyed this to me, I said that many of the teaching staff at The Lawrence School, Lovedale, and in particular Mr Srivalson, who used to teach Geography, had told me, "Your son is a gifted child, and that's why he is sometimes thrown out of class, for being inattentive." Ironic isn't it? But that is how life is. It brings to mind Raju Hirani's movie 3 Idiots. Déjà vu?

For the trust that we are running, we are presently focusing on primary and secondary education. To select students to be sponsored by the Foundation, we have laid down certain criteria. The main principal being that the child should be bright and keen to learn, but does not have adequate means. We do not want to sponsor any poor or underprivileged child. To find such children, who meet the criteria, is not easy. But somehow we get proposals for sponsorship when least expected. I am convinced beyond any doubt that this too is facilitated by Alyosha's soul.

On 29 August 2008, something happened that illustrates precisely this point. Except that in this instance, it was not I, but a total stranger, who I met on an aircraft, who felt as if Alyosha's spirit was present and sitting between us to enable a mentor for a girl called Komal Yadav, from Chaitanya School in Gandhinagar, Mumbai to be found. Her father, a peon in the same school had expired and being a bright child, she needed help to continue her education. That total stranger, Shubha Koshy, is a friend and a well-wisher of the Foundation today. Do read 'Catcher in the Rye' by Shubha Koshy in the 'Emails – From Alyosha's Friends' section of the book.

Similarly, on 30th September 2009, the second death anniversary of Alyosha, I received a call from the wife (who was then teaching in Army Public School at Noida) of an old colleague from the Navy and the submarines in particular. We hadn't been in touch ever since I had left the Navy over five years before that. After exchanging greetings, she came to the point and asked if the Foundation would sponsor a sepoy's son. His father had just expired. Incidentally, we had just completed the AGM of the trust a fortnight ago and were looking to extend the footprints of the Foundation, by finding some more students. Once again, to my mind, it was not a coincidence that on Alyosha's second death anniversary, a suitable proposal came forth out of the blue. The Foundation is now supporting the boy and he is doing very well. There have been many other smaller incidents, which lead us to believe that his soul is watching over us and facilitating events so that his vision is realised.

In a reflective mood

~12 ~

The Spiritual Soul - II

The fourth anniversary

In September 2011, his fourth "shradh" fell on the 19th of the month. As usual, we had the prayer ceremony at our home in Pune. However, it is said that on the fourth shradh during the "pitra paksha", a fortnightly period in the month of shradh (usually falling in September), if a 'pind daan' ritual is conducted in the holy city of Gaya, then no further shradhs need be performed. We had accordingly planned to travel to Gaya for the said purpose. Four of us, I, my sister, my wife and her youngest sister were to travel. We were to fly from Mumbai on the 23rd and take the New Delhi-Bhuvaneshwar Rajdhani Express the same evening so as to reach Gaya early next morning.

I had heard that in a city like Gaya, when one landed up during the shradh month, all kinds of 'pandas' would crowd around you, each promising to conduct the rituals to ensure eternal peace for the departed soul. Their demands of fees and the materials required can be very irritating and many get put off totally. In order to avoid all this hassle, I had arranged through my army course mates to have us received and accommodated in a service mess. Arrangements were therefore made in a NCC mess at Gaya and fortuitously, a service priest was also available, who was competent to conduct the 'pind daan' ritual. Since we were there on a weekend, he could attend to us without in any manner being taken away from his duties.

My wife had made the train reservations to Gaya and back for all of us at different times. Yet somehow all four of us got berths in the same four-bunker compartment, even though two of us were in the wait list/RAC. It never usually happens.

We took the flight from Mumbai to Delhi on the morning of 23rd September. After settling down in the aircraft and on completion of boarding, the air hostess made the usual welcome announcement. When she told us that the name of the captain of the aircraft was Captain Mukeshwaran, we got goose pimples. It could not have been a coincidence. It needs to be recalled that Alyosha had named his labrador pet Brutus, but never again called him by that name. Instead he always called him Mukeshwaran. On hearing that the captain of the aircraft had the same name, which is a highly uncommon name, I said to my wife that Alyosha's soul was accompanying us and that everything on the trip would go off smoothly.

On arrival at Gaya in the early hours on

24th September 2011, we were received and taken to the NCC mess, where we were informed that the panditji would come to meet us at 10am. That allowed us to catch some much needed sleep. The gentleman came to meet us at the appointed time and we firmed up the programme for the ritual next morning. He was particularly keen that we reach the 'vishnu pada' temple by 7am, as he feared that later we would not get any place to carry out the rituals. Such was the rush.

As planned, we reached the temple exactly at the desired time, but even the pandit had underestimated the rush. We could not find any spot in the open courtyard around the temple where the five of us could sit. Eventually, we found some corner space just next to the entrance to the sanctum sanctorum but it was very dirty. It was also protected from the skies by the overhanging roof of the entrance. The priest told us to wait as he went to find a cleaner. At this moment, I just turned around and found a person with a bamboo broom who asked if I wanted that place cleaned. I could have sworn that we had not seen him around anywhere till that moment. I nodded and he did his job and just vanished. He could not be seen anywhere in the temple premises later either. Very unusual as such persons hang around to make a living. In a few minutes, the panditji returned and found that the place had already been cleaned. We all sat down and the rituals were soon started. As soon as we commenced the puja, it started raining and all the other folks who were seated in the open courtyard for their rituals rushed to find shelter, whereas we could continue without hindrance due to the protection of the overhang of the roof. It took us about an hour to finish and it rained the entire time. As soon as we completed the puja, it stopped raining. Was it a strange coincidence? Even if I chose, I would rather think not. To all of us the events had unfolded as if a force had facilitated them. The sudden appearance and disappearance of the cleaner, the only vacant spot at a vantage position sheltered from rain which lasted the exact duration of our ritual were all occurrences out of the ordinary and seemed as if some power was facilitating all this.

On this visit, there was more. After we had finished the shradh, we returned to the mess and thereafter the panditji took us around Gaya to visit some more holy spots, during which the weather held. No sooner than we returned to the mess and finished our lunch, it started raining heavily. We were confined to our cabins as even going for a walk was not possible. We switched on the television and learnt that it was raining heavily in that part of the country and that the rail tracks at Mughalsarai junction, which is two hours from Gaya and falls on the main trunk route from Howrah to New Delhi were under water. There was no certainty as to when the services would be restored. We had to take the train that night from

Gaya to New Delhi and had important appointments to keep. (My sister-in-law, Sabena had a flight to Mumbai; my sister and I had a very important appointment to keep in the Ministry of Home Affairs regarding the Foundation). We were really praying that normalcy in the train operations would get restored, but given the news reports till evening it was looking unlikely. My wife told us not to worry and that we would roll in at New Delhi Station bang on schedule at 10 am the next day. She felt confident because from the moment we had boarded the aircraft in Mumbai, she felt that Alyosha's soul was guiding us.

Our train from Gaya – the Rajdhani Express from Bhuvaneshwar to New Delhi – arrived at Gaya on schedule at 11.15, as that route was not affected. Our next stop was at Mughalsarai, where services were disrupted. We were to reach there at 01.15 h. However, soon after boarding the train, we went off to sleep leaving everything to fate. On waking up the next morning, we learnt that we were just about 30 minutes late but that too was made up as we rolled into New Delhi station exactly on schedule. This had seemed virtually impossible the night before. It was as if some divine force was at work.

Visiting the Lawrence School, Lovedale

Another incident that comes to mind occurred in May 2011. Deepa and I had gone to Bangalore in connection with the trial of Alyosha's assassins and had to meet the Special Public Prosecutor as well as our lawyer. We had planned to stay there for two days there and then leave by train for Coimbatore. From there we were due to go to Lovedale by road on 5 May to attend the Founder's Day celebrations at the Lawrence School the next day. As it turned out our train tickets were still not confirmed the night before and Deepa's knee, which had been giving her trouble got even worse, so we cancelled the tickets and decided to travel to Lovedale, some 300kms away, by taxi.

En-route, we passed through Sringapatnam, just short of Mysore where the sangam of South India happens – that is the confluence of three rivers, Kaveri, Kabini and Hemavati. It is a sacred and holy place and is also a 'vishnu sthala'. We had in October 2007, immersed one part of Alyosha's ashes or 'asthi' at this sangam. Since it was on the way, Deepa suggested that we take a short detour and visit the place. On reaching there, we took a dip in the river and once again paid our homage to Alyosha's soul. No sooner had we finished and sat in the taxi to be on our way to Lovedale, Deepa felt totally free from the pain in her knee. It was as if Alyosha had guided us to take this route and that the dip in the river had cured her.

We reached the Lawrence School, Lovedale the same afternoon and handed over the award scholarship cheque for the Best All-Round student in prep School 2010-11 to the Deputy Headmistress as well as the certificate that goes with it. The next day we attended the Founder's Day Parade and the award ceremony thereafter. This was the first time we were visiting the school after Alyosha had left in the summer of 1998.

Much had changed. The old Junior School dormitories had been demolished and new modern rooms were nearing completion. At the award ceremony, we met Alyosha's old English teacher Ms Wirk, who was happy to meet us but also sad to have lost one of her best students in Alyosha. We shared Alyosha's will with her and she was amazed that he had written it when he was in Prep School. We also met the matron from the Prep School who used to look after the children there. She was overwhelmed to meet us and remembered Alyosha very fondly. It really brought us to tears to learn that Alyosha had left an indelible mark on whoever he had interacted with. We visited the dorms in the Prep School and the Senior School; also saw the Junior School, the Top Flats, the Science Block etc and all the other places that he would frequent his schooling years. We also met Sagarika Das, who had won the Alyosha Kumar Award scholarship that year. It was nostalgic and a cathartic experience for us.

Old Souls

Alyosha was very fond of Aruna, who was his mother's close friend. He used to call her maasi, meaning mother's sister. Her two children were with him in Lawrence School, though senior in years. They were like family to him and during our visits to Lovedale for Founder's Day, we would spend time together. Alyosha would often share secrets with Aruna that he would not with us, his parents. After he passed, Aruna would tell us that she often saw him in her dreams and they would talk. In one such dream, which was sometime in early February 2008, she saw him getting an apartment ready. He was engaged in furnishing it as well as putting away his mother's clothes in the wardrobes. She asked him what he was up to. He replied "Maasi, more often than not I only cause my mother anguish, so this time before she moves in, I thought of settling the apartment. At least once I must make her happy". It so happened that when we moved back to Dubai from Moscow after his demise, we had moved into an apartment quite similar to the one Aruna had seen in her dream. Coincidentally, I had ensured that before my wife moved in, it was fully settled and she did not have to lift a finger. We had a photo of Alyosha in each room of the apartment and from each; it appeared that his eyes followed us through the house. His soul seemed to be always watching over us and guide us in moments of stress. It is he who gives us the strength to carry on with life.

Towards his later years, in my interaction with Alyosha, I could sense that he was showing his spiritual side in a more pronounced manner. Even in a testimonial he wrote on his roommate at NLS, Nimesh Guru, this facet was evident. I reproduce the text here. "Nimesh is a deeply humane and spiritual man, which is why I think we share great affinity. He is also very ambitious, which does not go well with the other side of him and makes him frustrated. We have a constant dialectic to decide if life is ultimately good and meaningful (me) or pointless and predetermined (him). Neither wins, but I think we both have rubbed off on each other a little. I still like Nimesh very much though, and hope he realizes that the elixir he seeks is already within him." There is no doubt that Alyosha was a highly perceptive person and believed in the innate goodness of others.

The chakradhari

Alyosha was a 'chakradhari' by birth. A 'chakradhari', as I was told by a palmist, is a person who has, on all his fingers, a perfect chakra of prints. Normally, a person's fingerprints won't have complete concentric circles on all ten fingers of the hands. Rarely does one come across a person with complete whorls on their fingers. It signifies a fiercely independent mind and will, and non-conformism. Chakradharis test everything through the prism of their own intelligence. They are also believed to be incarnates of Vishnu; the word chakradhar is another name for Vishnu. I do not claim that Alyosha was one, but what he had on his forehead since birth – a natural sign – was the 'Vishnu Chinha' or the mark of Vishnu, the Letter 'u' of the Roman script. This can be seen in the photograph on next page. We have shown this photograph to many priest and pundits. All of them were quite surprised, but said the same thing: the mark of Vishnu on Alyosha's forehead signified that he was in a way an incarnation of Vishnu, and here in this world only for a specific purpose and time to liberate himself from the cycle of birth and death.

There are some other photographs of Alyosha's taken in his last years. All of them have a distinct light on the forehead, even in company, which negates a reflection of the camera flash.

Vishnu mark on forehead is natural

Alyoshasaint

In March 2006, he changed his email ID and sent an email to a chosen few. He wrote: "This is Alyosha Kumar's new e-mail address. Mail it liberally with lots of confidence of getting replies, sou moto mails etc. 'Alyoshasaint' is the name for the new avatar. Yours for constant contact, Alyosha." What prompted him to call himself a saint is a mystery to us. We must have read and laughed it off, as we had done with his will. However, after his tragic demise, we started discovering more about the evolved nature of his spirit and soul through peers, colleagues and friends. Mostly, parents are blinded by affection and do not see the real person their child is. It is sudden jolts like this one that force one to look beyond the veneer. Tradition bound, we saw him as a maverick much as others in his circle of influence did. Now I know that he was very different and special. Whenever anyone spoke to him or engaged him in a discussion or debate, he would always have an impish smile and an expression, which suggested that: "Hey, I know all this but am talking along to humour you and to give due respect to your views."

In Russian, Alyosha is the pet name of Alexey. As I said earlier, Alyosha was very fond of the Russian author Dostoyevsky, and his classic The Brothers Karamazov was his favourite book. The main protagonist in that book is also Alyosha, a religious character. I'm not sure if Alyosha identified himself with the character in the book. I found a passage in the chapter 'Of the Holy Scriptures in the life of Father Zosima', which I reproduce here: "And there is no need of much teaching and explanation, he will understand it all simply. Do you suppose that the peasants don't understand? Try reading them the touching story of the fair Esther and the haughty Vashti; or the miraculous story of Jonah in the whale. Don't forget the parables of Our Lord, choose especially from the Gospel of St Luke and then from the Acts of the Apostles the conversion of St Paul, and from the lives of Saints, for instance, the life of Alexey, the man of God and, greatest of all, the happy martyr and the seer of god, Mary of Egypt." Alyosha too was martyred defending the honour of his friend.

Was Alyosha a divine soul? We can't be sure. Still, the circumstances, events and the physical signs on his person do suggest it.

A colleague and very dear friend of mine died in 2004, when he was just 52. His father gave me this poem 'I'll Lend You a Child' by Edgar Guest saying that it would give us solace. I reproduce it here:

"I will lend you for a little time, a child of mine," He said,
It may be six or seven years, or twenty two or three,
But will you till I call him back, take care of him for me?
He will bring his charms to gladden you and should his stay be brief,
You will have his lovely memories as solace for your grief.

I cannot promise he will stay, since all from Earth must return,
But there are lessons taught down there, I want this child to learn.
I have looked this world over, in my search for teachers true,
And from the throngs that crowd the lanes, I have chosen you.
Now will you give him all your love, not think labour vain,
Nor hate me when I come to call, and take him back again?
I fancied that I heard them say, "Dear Lord Thy will be done,
For all the joy Thy child shall bring, the risk of grief will run.
We will shelter him with tenderness; we will love him while we may,
And for the happiness we have known forever grateful stay.
But should the angels call for him, much sooner than we planned,
We will have the bitter grief that comes, and try to understand."

Reading it we were so overwhelmed because it really reflected the circumstances and the story of Alyosha. My wife and I are now convinced that Alyosha was a gift to us, in the real sense, from the Almighty. He was sent to complete his remaining karma to attain salvation. We were fortunate to have been chosen as his parents and he was a blessing in our lives.

Of course, even after his death he is ensuring that we continue to do good by the society as per his desire to help the poor using his money through the Foundation. All those who know us, will vouch that we in fact fulfilled 'The God's Will'. We gave him the best of education;

the values that he needed to imbibe, and unfettered freedom and love. His mother was totally devoted in his upbringing. He would often tell her "Mamma, you are so different from others and I am really fortunate and blessed to have you for a mom." Little did he know that in fact, he was the blessing in our lives. To lose one's only progeny and at such a young age is the biggest tragedy that any parent can suffer. However, given all that we have learnt of Alyosha, we feel privileged to have had him as our son. He was taken away by the Almighty as the angel's share. Still, we need to celebrate his life rather than grieve for him. He inspired so many when he was alive and continues to do so even after his death.

The Student

Early Childhood

Alyosha was a born genius. His IQ was in the 150s. Even as infant, one could see the light in his eyes, which in a sense I believe reflected his innate intelligence. It is believed that a child's education starts from the womb itself, whilst that is an issue in which many frontiers are yet to be opened, I know for certain that an infant starts imbibing all that is around him/her from the very first instant that he/she comes into this world.

For the first three months of his life, Alyosha stayed in a maternity hospital in Vladivostok (Russia) with his mother, who had postnatal trauma in the form of a ruptured pubic Symphysis. During this period, he was cared for by a dedicated nurse as also by all the other patients in the ward adjacent to the room where he and his mother were kept. He would be subjected to all types of conversations in Russian, Hindi and English. How much of it disseminated into his infant brain is difficult to say, but it all contributed to his growth and his initiation into the world of words and sounds. Having seen him in his years later on, from a toddler to a super intelligent young man, I have no doubt that his education was started in that hospital itself.

Due to his mother's medical condition, both had to come back to India in the summer of 1985, when Alyosha was just six months old. In Mumbai, where they took up residence in one of the Naval Officer's flats, Colaba, he was fortunate to be among his aunts, both maternal and paternal and his cousins.

I returned to Mumbai on completing my assignment in April 1986. This period of ten months was one of consolidation of Alyosha's education. In a way, his mother's medical recovery period was a boon for him, as everyone around him went out of their way to focus their energies and attention on him.

When I got back in April 1986, Alyosha was barely 16 months, but was conversing well. He refused to call me Papa, instead addressing me by my name Arun. This, of course, lasted only for a year or so, after which he was back to calling me Papa. I guess he needed reassurance that his father had come back to be with him for good.

In his infancy and toddler years, he was subjected to the usual stories for children, especially prior to turning in at night. These have their own effect in channelising the thought processes and growth of a child's brain. What was remarkable in Alyosha's case was that he would retain it all with focused clarity. Books such as Captain Courageous, Jack and the Beanstalk, Treasure Island etc.

In the 1980s, in India, there weren't such a plethora of TV channels as in present times. There was only Doordarshan (DD), the AIR channel – even the second DD channel came into being much later, running serials such as Yeh Jo Hai Zindagi, Buniyaad etc. (These became classics in a way.) His mother was fond of them and Alyosha would watch them too. It was really extraordinary that this 20-month-old child could follow the theme of Buniyaad, which was a story related to the Partition of India.

We, as parents, apart from the usual kindergarten stuff, would also read him stories from Panchantra, Amar Chitra Katha, as also from abridged English classics such as mentioned above. This, I am convinced, had a profound impact on him, and instilled in him both curiosity and a reading habit, which was so much in evidence in his later life. In school, as a rule, he would try and finish two books a month, which increased to two a week, later on.

Another significant aspect that likely impacted his intellectual growth and general awareness was the travel that he experienced in his early years. By the time he was four, he had travelled extensively, within India and abroad to the Far East (Japan, Hong Kong, Thailand) and the Persian Gulf (Bahrain). This exposure to information and awareness, through books and travel led to his ability to imbibe the essence of his environment. My being in the Navy meant frequent transfers, and consequently a lot of travel and seeing different places. While this can broaden a young person's worldview, for a school-going child it can also lead to adjustment problems, with schools changing every two to three years. This paradox is faced by every person in uniform.

I was very fortunate and privileged to have had a very erudite and scholarly father. I have yet to meet someone like him. He was a lawyer by education and a political scientist, but through his readings also a historian, a linguist, a mathematician and a social scientist. He had a great influence on me. Alyosha too was fortunate to have interacted with him. My father lived with us in his final years, from 1986 to 1993 when he passed away. Alyosha's reading habit was, in a great part, thanks to my father. As has been noted in a different chapter, my father had presented him the complete works of Shakespeare and Charles Dickens, and Alyosha had finished reading most of it by the age of 13. These books must have had an effect on his thoughts about society in particular and humanity in general. He did demonstrate a charitable disposition, a definite Dickensian leaning.

He also got basic lessons in geometry and trigonometry from my father during 1992-93, when

Alyosha was in the third standard. This was not forced upon him, but put across in a very natural way by using common examples such as finding the width of a river using a high object on its banks, and the angles. This kindled his curiosity and it is no wonder that Alyosha excelled in mathematics in school. In fact after his grandfather's demise in May 1993, Alyosha did not give in to tears, but all he asked was: "Now, who will teach me maths?" He had grown much attached to his grandfather, in particular due to my father always passing on pearls of wisdom to him.

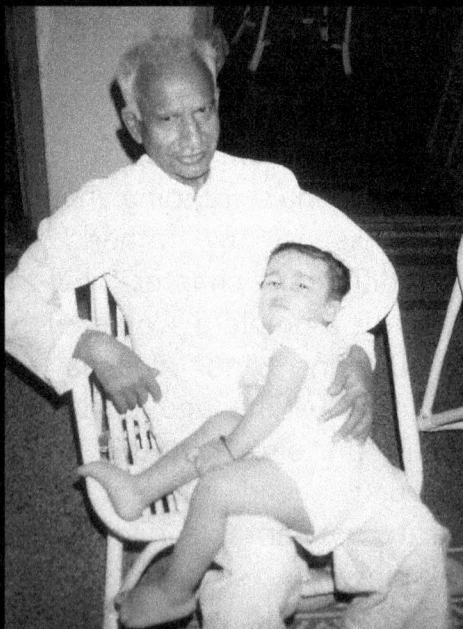

With his grand father

Alyosha had a fascination for numbers and sensing this, we encouraged him to dabble in them. His aunt Sabena gifted him a mini-math computer game. In the Eighties, home computers were just making an appearance in India. However, this gadget would pose questions on number series, their patterns and on progressions, wherein one was required to find the missing number in the sequence or series. Alyosha would invariably come up with the right answer. It was then that I realized that we had a gifted mind at hand.

The School Years

Alyosha's formal schooling started in Visakhapatnam in early 1988 in a play school called Tiny Tots, located within the naval officer's residential area called Naval Park. I had once again gone off to Russia, as part of the commissioning crew of INS Chakra.

I was glad to see that at Tiny Tots, children were allowed to bloom naturally. In Alyosha's case, given his innate intelligence, he was able to imbibe basic lessons from his surroundings very clearly. In the kindergarten years, Alyosha was way ahead of his contemporaries. His understanding of natural shapes, colours and apprehensions of his environment was truly remarkable. After I had returned, I used to frequently interact with one of his teachers, Mrs Prasad, who was a naval wife. Alyosha was rather fond of her.

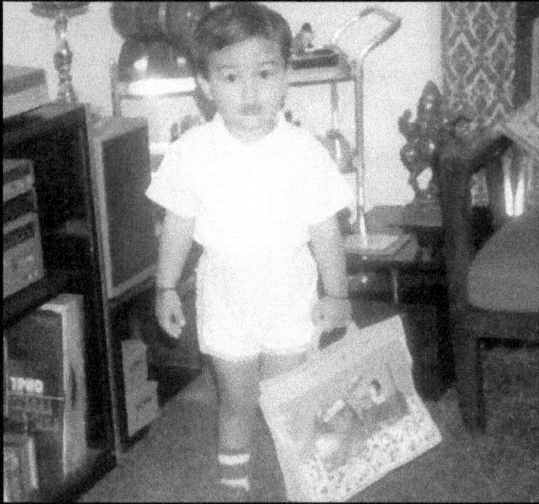
Ready for KG

During the two years that he spent in KG, Alyosha enjoyed himself. Never once did he cry when being sent to school. Towards the latter half, the school did introduce the children to writing, which for me, personally, was still early as I believed that toddlers shouldn't be taught formally before the age of five, but I was persuaded to go along. The good part was that the children were exposed to a lot of extra-curricular activities. In one of the school functions, he had played the role of a screen-wiper of a bus in the nursery rhyme "The wheels of the bus go round and round". The following year, he played a barber in a similar nursery rhyme. These exposures nurtured his self-confidence a great deal and he did not show any stage fright at all, which was to stand him in good stead in his later years at school.

His first school was Naval Public in Visakhapatnam where he joined in the first standard in 1990. His preparation at Tiny Tots and at home had set him up well for school. His ability to comprehend and grasp were clearly evident and he was ahead of his class. I remember my submarine was deployed to Mumbai from our base Visakhapatnam for three months. After a month, I requested my wife to join me there. The problem was Alyosha's school, but his teacher permitted him to take a month off as she felt he could afford to miss that period since he was much ahead of his class. Needless to say, at the end of the annual exams that year, he topped his class.

In June 1991, we had to shift to Wellington (Coonoor in the Nilgiri hills) as I was deputed to the Defence Services Staff College. For me, it was rather late in my career to attend the course, as most of the directing staff were either contemporaries or juniors. But I could not have completed it earlier as I had been away in Russia with the Nuclear Submarine Project – I ended up as the second in command of the INS Chakra before the boat was returned once the lease expired – and could not have been spared.

After we reached Wellington in the middle of June 1991, and settled down in the house allotted to us, we had to search for a good school. Usually most officer students put their children in a convent school, 'Holy Innocents,' which was located amidst the married accommodations area at Gorkha hills. However, we visited a day-boarding school called St Joseph's Anglo-Indian High School for Boys which was just a couple of kilometers enroute to lower Coonoor. It was a traditional school, little over a century old, founded in 1888, with a sprawling campus. Alyosha took an instant fancy to the school, more so because it had a full-sized football ground among other sports fields. He loved football and decided that it was this school that he wanted to study in during our stay in Wellington, which was to be only for a year.

He joined in the second standard and soon enough made his presence felt in the class as well as in the school. He was at the top of his class. He was extremely fortunate to have as his teacher a very warm, competent and affectionate Anglo-Indian lady, Angela Beale. Her husband, Derryck, also taught there. (Later he started his own school in Gudalur for poor children. Sadly, he passed away in the autumn of 2011). Alyosha became so fond of her that, for him, she remained his favourite teacher. Even when he was at Lawrence School, Lovedale and the Law School at Bangalore, in later years, he would make it a point to visit her in Coonoor at least once a year.

Alyosha with Ms Angela Beale

Alyosha was always well-behaved at home and had very few demands for a kid his age, so we always thought of him as the quiet, obedient sort. My wife and I remember having a chat with Angela once in St Joseph's and saying that managing Alyosha was quite a simple affair. She at once retorted: "Oh he can be quite a rascal, but a loving one". We all laughed it away and only then did we, as parents, realize that Alyosha reserved all his mischief for school. His stay at St Joseph's was very eventful. He did extremely well in academics as well as in extra-curricular activities. Before the winter break for Christmas, he won the fancy dress competition in school, dressed as Santa Claus. I am convinced that it was not so much the dress itself but the manner in which he presented himself before the audience that carried the day for him. He spoke with extreme confidence, greeted the children as Santa would, bringing with him all his presents.

As Santa Claus

In May 1992, we were posted to Mumbai on completion of the staff course. Alyosha had been judged the best all-round student in the second standard and was awarded a shield for it. The day we were to leave, he just disappeared, just when we were set to drive away from Coonoor. Worried as we were at his sudden disappearance, we anxiously waited for an hour till he fetched up. He had walked down to say farewell to his favourite teacher Angela. That we would be anxious and worried by his absence never even occurred to him. He was like that. The Foundation that we run in his memory has instituted an award scholarship at St Joseph's School, for the 'Best All-Round Student' in the second standard.

We drove down from Wellington to Mumbai. En route, we visited Trivandrum, Kovalam beach, Cochin, and up along the coastal National Highway 17 right up to Mumbai, we stopped at Kannur, Mangalore, Karwar, Goa and Chiplun. The drive itself was a great learning experiences for Alyosha, who was a young 7 ½ year-old boy. In all these towns, there were sites of historical significance which added to the knowledge of the young mind. We reached Mumbai after having been on the road for ten days. It was a very enriching experience, especially seeing the Chinese fishing nets at the entrance to Cochin harbour and tasting different cuisines along the way.

Bombay

Once we had settled down, shacking up with a friend and colleague in Mumbai, the search for a school for Alyosha began. To get admission to a good school was a real problem as most schools preferred locals and one needed to pull some ropes to find a seat in a good school. Although I did try, and received a call from the Cathedral and John Connon School, Alyosha would have none of it and said that he would rather attend the Naval School, which operated out of a limited campus in 1992 (now it has a much larger area). He told me that he did not care much for the snobbish value of such schools. Seeing that this difficulty would arise every time I got transferred, we decided to admit him to a residential school in due course. Whilst at Wellington, I was the local guardian of a boy at Lawrence School, Lovedale and had made many a visit there. Alyosha was very impressed with the school, so in 1992 I made a special trip to register him for admission from the fifth standard. To get admission however, Alyosha would have to appear for an entrance test, which was still a year and half away.

Eventually, we put Alyosha in the Naval School in Mumbai. He did standard three and four there and as was his wont, topped in academics. He also joined the Bharat scouts and guides, which gave him good exposure to both adventure and the concept of social service. Although, Alyosha was a born footballer, it was during this period that he honed his skills. We used to stay in Dhanraj Mahal, next to Regal Cinema at Apollo Bunder. Our Secretary there, Commander Vadhera had got a hard square made, where the children could play basketball as well as football. During his stay in Mumbai, he also picked up golf and in a few short months was cracking in the nineties.

Alyosha continued with his general reading and as a consequence his general awareness was truly remarkable for a boy his age. He would also question everything and one had to give him answers that would satisfy him. I remember one such occasion. He asked: "Why does a ship made of iron float, when iron is heavier than water"? This was when he was in the third standard. Not wanting to tax his mind with understanding Archimedes' Principle, I simplified it and told him: "Because it has got air in it." It was a valid explanation to my mind since the volume of the watertight compartments constitute the displacement of the ship.

One day on getting back from school, he waited for me till I got back from work in the evening, looking very upset. The first thing he asked me was: "Why did you tell me a lie?" As it happened, his class teacher had posed the same question in class and only Alyosha had volunteered to answer. Naturally, he gave the answer that his father had given him. The teacher, a naval officer's wife, laughed at it and said: "What rubbish? It floats because of the way it is shaped". Being rebuked in front of his peers hurt him and so he confronted me at the first available chance. I then said that I had told him the correct thing and proceeded to explain Archimedes' principle to him, using a glass tumbler with varying levels of water in it and floating it in a basin. He grasped that it was the volume of the tumbler that made it effectively lighter than the water, even though glass is heavier, similar to a ship made of iron.

I then demonstrated to him that if the water displaced by the tumbler was equal in weight to that of the tumbler (with some water in it), then the tumbler would float. I suggested he imagine the tumbler to be the ship, the water in it the machinery and occupied volume, and the balance as free volume of air. Thus a ship made of iron would float similarly. He completely understood it and said that he would talk to the teacher in class the next day. I told him that I would give him a letter for the teacher, which I did. In that letter I explained the same principle and also asserted that rebuking a student in class when he had sought to answer a difficult question was just not done. He had given the right answer and I suggested to the teacher that she explain the answer to the whole class as if coming from her, and that she had erred in understanding Alyosha's answer. I must candidly say that the teacher graciously fulfilled my suggestion. This helped in restoring Alyosha's confidence and his standing among his peers.

I have mentioned this incident also to highlight that an inquisitive child must be encouraged to question. Sadly in our educational system in India, the focus is only on learning by rote. The entire process needs an overhaul. Only then can we bring up a generation that is well equipped to deal with the unexpected problems and situations life throws at us.

The Lawrence School Years

Alyosha completed his third and fourth standard from the naval school in Mumbai. In November 1993 he appeared for the entrance examination for the Lawrence School, Lovedale. In February 1994, we were informed the he had cleared the entrance test and was required to join the school in by mid-April. I did not know it then, but Dev Lahiri, who was the Headmaster there at that time, told me after Alyosha's tragic passing away in September 2007 that he had topped the entrance test.

Thus began his tryst with Lawrence School, Lovedale, a school he really loved. He joined the Prep School (fourth, fifth and sixth standards) in April 1994. The school is located at Lovedale at a height of 2,200 mts in the Nilgiri hills, 4kms short of the hill station Udhaga Mandalam, more famously known as 'Ooty', in the state of Tamil Nadu.

It was founded in 1858 by Sir Major General Henry Lawrence, as an asylum for the children of British officers and soldiers in India during the colonial rule. After Independence, the governance of all the Lawrence schools (now there are only two – one at Lovedale and the second at Sanawar, in Kasuali near Simla) became the responsibility of the Union Ministry of Education now known as the Ministry of Human Resources Development. The Secretary, Ministry of HRD is the Chairman of the Governing Board. However, the school does not get any aid/grants from the Union Government and is totally funded through its own resources and revenues. It has a campus of 700 acres (with an active campus of 45 acres) for 700 students, which amounts to one acre per child. It is a co-ed residential school, with great traditions and record. The maximum temperature is about 24°C, and in winters it falls to nearly zero. It's a great ambience with plenty of fresh air that allows children to grow up in a very healthy environment.

In Alyosha's education and the development of his personality, this school played the most important part. He blossomed here into a fine, intelligent young man. His mother and aunt Sabena had gone to drop him at Lovedale in April 1994. I was busy doing the Naval Higher Command Course in Mumbai. After they had admitted him and settled him down in the dormitory at the Prep School, he wanted them to leave immediately, whereas in most cases, children want their mothers to hang on for as long as possible. When they visited him the next day, before returning to Mumbai, he asked: "Why have you come?" This was most unusual.

He settled down quickly and did very well in his curriculum. In early May, Deepa and I went to the school for Founder's Day and were extremely satisfied that Alyosha had taken to the school and he was well appreciated by his house staff as well as his teachers. In fact his Prep School Headmaster, Mr Raghavan (now deceased) told us that he was very happy with Alyosha's performance and rated him as a very intelligent and inquisitive student. He would question everything. This was not news to us, but we were only concerned that it be viewed in the right perspective and we were glad that it was so.

Often I have wondered that in our country we have schools for physically and mentally challenged children, but there are none to cater to exceptionally bright and gifted children. Such children more often than not become disinterested in the classes as they have already moved ahead of their classmates and teachers find it difficult to get them to be attentive in class. I sincerely feel that this aspect needs consideration so that the gift of such children can be nurtured and channelized appropriately.

In his class at the Prep School, Mr Raghavan, who apart from being the mathematics teacher and the Prep School's headmaster, would hold a weekly quiz competition called the 'Mathematician of the week'. Alyosha's class fellow Celina Stephen, who has been mentioned in the chapter: "Alyosha and the Little Prince", wrote to me to say: 'Alyosha's love for mathematics had always amazed me. I was terrible at it. We used to have a quiz at the end of every week for which he always managed to grab the title of 'Mathematician of the week'.

Like all such residential schools, the thrust was not merely on academics, but on all-round development of the students. The vast campus afforded adequate space for play grounds, cross country tracks, hikes and treks and other outdoor activities including riding.

The extra-curricular activities also included music, arts and crafts, sculpture, a school band, dramatics, elocution etc. The daily regime was quite taxing. Reveille at 6 AM and lights out at 10pm. The children were kept busy the whole day. This was another reason to send Alyosha to such a school, as realizing his gift, we felt that he would be kept gainfully occupied and that his inquisitive mind would not run wild.

Here he got the full opportunity to express himself in all spheres. He excelled in academics and stood first in his class for the four out of five years he spent in the school. He won the prestigious Mahindra Scholarship award of Rs 5,000/ in 1997 for having stood first for three consecutive years. It was a princely sum for him and he was really proud of it – literally his first earnings. He excelled in equal measure in sports, particularly in football. He was also part of the Junior Under-13 cricket team (as wicket keeper-batsman) that won the Nilgiri District Trophy for two years in succession. It was in Lawrence School that his love for basketball was actually born, which would flourish later in Law School. He also avidly took to cross country during his stay here, which stood him in good stead in keeping himself fit later on.

In fact his performance in the Prep School had surely marked him out to become the head boy in the sixth standard but he did not, the story of which has been narrated in the chapter 'Alyosha and The Little Prince'. That was due to his absolute honesty.

Alyosha had a compassionate nature, and that is reflected in his will, which He wrote this during a prep period in the 5th Std, an evening before being admitted to the school hospital on account of chicken pox. He was most helpful to other students in helping them out with their studies, but cleverly had also made it profitable for himself by taking tuck-vouchers from them.

He was a voracious reader and his general knowledge was exceptional. Those days there was no internet and TV channels were also limited. His knowledge came from his reading. So it was natural for him to be selected to represent the school in the Bournvita Quiz Contest, telecast in November 1997, though the recording had been done in August of the same year. He and his team partner reached the semifinals at the national level and missed making it to the final by a whisker.

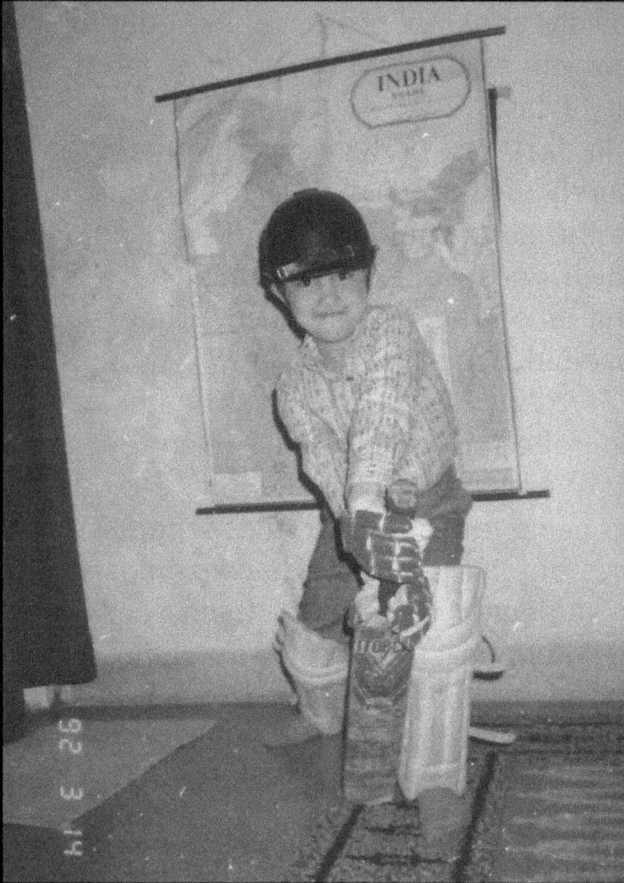
Alyosha in cricket gear

He had joined the school band initially as a side drummer, but later changed to the bugle. His favourite score in the band was the classic "When the Saints Go Marching In". This used to be the entry score for the band on to the parade ground, during the Founder's Day ceremonial parade. (Alyosha also loved the Beatles and old Hindi film songs. He was also a great fan of karaoke nights.)

Despite being an outstanding student, Alyosha was not a nerd. He would make mischief and play pranks on his classmates. One such incident is narrated by Celina. She wrote: "Out of all the instances, I remember one very clearly. One morning before tea break we had a computer class where we weren't allowed to enter the lab with our shoes. We had to line them up on the shelves just outside the lab. To my surprise, when the class was over I found my pair missing. I spent the entire tea break searching for my shoes in the corridor. After I gave up searching, I noticed a pair that was still lying on the shelves but they definitely weren't mine. I had to find out whose pair it was since he/she had to be wearing mine!!!

I stumbled my way to class with the ill-fitting shoe in the hope of finding my own. I was obviously late for class and was made to give an explanation for the delay. My language teacher announced to the class to check their shoes. I noticed Alyosha in the corner of the class with a sheepish grin on his face and immediately knew where to find my shoes (I don't know how he managed to fit into them). I walked up to him and asked him to return my shoes immediately. The whole class burst into laughter. He very innocently said that he hadn't realized it and was sorry, but later admitted that he had done so just to play a prank on me".

Correspondence with parents was compulsory and students were to write home once a week. However I used to write to Alyosha daily just to have a vibrant communication channel with him. He once asked me: "Why do you write daily? I cannot reply to each letter". I told him that I did not expect a reply to each letter and that he should write as and when he had the time. The idea was to let him know that he was constantly in our thoughts. There were no mobile phones and parents were not permitted to speak to the children on the landlines of the school, except in an emergency.

I remember a couple of incidents in school, which reveal something about the kind of personality Alyosha was. I was in Kochi, doing a pre-commissioning training to take over command of a guided missile destroyer. On alternate weekends I would travel to Lovedale to catch up with Alyosha. On one such visit, I reached the school on a Saturday afternoon and found out that Alyosha was in French class. I walked up to the classroom when the class was breaking, but our friend was not to be seen. One of his class mates told me that Alyosha had been turned out of the class halfway through the period. I was quite taken aback and was at a loss as to where to find him. Just then I ran into Mr Srivalson, who used to teach geography and was also a housemaster. When I mentioned this to him he said "Captain Kumar, your son is a gifted child and that is why he is sometimes turned out of the class. Not everyone understands him and often his questions are taken amiss. You should be prepared for this." His words were prophetic, because in Law School, Alyosha faced this situation several times. I eventually found Alyosha playing basketball all by himself in the Junior School courtyard.

The second incident worth recalling happened with his English teacher in Junior School, Ms Rao. After seeing off Alyosha to his dormitory I was heading out of the school, when I bumped into Ms Rao. She walked up to me and said "Captain Kumar, your son is not being attentive in my class. He keeps looking out of the window". I told her: "Ms Rao, that is your problem and not mine. You are his teacher and how to keep him engaged is solely dependent on you. However, I know what you mean, but my guess is that he has already moved ahead, hence the non-attentiveness. May I suggest that you give him books to read and ask him to write reviews on them? I promise that you won't have any further problems with him". She agreed and as I had anticipated, I did not hear any more complaints from her. This incidents highlight that usually there are no problem students, but that students may have problems, which if rightly identified, can be resolved.

In Blue Patrols, the rig for the ceremonial parade

The National Law School, Bangalore

The five-year stay in the National Law School (NLS) was to be the most crucial and decisive period for Alyosha's future. In hindsight, it turned out precisely so, although it had a most unfortunate ending.

Although Alyosha had studied at a residential school, being in a residential college was going to be a challenge because there is far less supervision and greater temptations. Added to this is the age when one is growing out of adolescence into adulthood. This period requires a great deal of sensitivity and handling on the part of parents and the hostel wardens in the institution. In most residential colleges, the Director and the Registrar usually live on the campus to keep a tab on what's happening. That is how it was at the NLS when it was founded and during the tenure of Mr Madhava Menon, who was the Founding Director. The situation changed only when Mr Jay Govind, who earlier was a professor, was appointed the Officiating Director when Mr Mohan Gopal resigned in 2003. Both the Director and the Registrar were not living on campus and it had its consequences, mostly negative as regards discipline and general wellbeing of the students. Once this happens, it is usually very difficult to pull back the ropes and regain control.

Alyosha had settled in quite nicely and performed exceedingly well in the first trimester, scoring the maximum in economics in his class. But being accident prone, he sure enough injured himself within two months of joining. Apparently, after a strenuous run, he collapsed in the shower rooms and hit his head on the edge of the sink. When informed, we were not perturbed as this was not something new for us. I did manage a trip to Bangalore after the incident to see him and all seemed well. The law school had a trimester system – July to September with a 15-day break in October; then mid-Oct to mid-Jan; and then a third trimester from mid-March to mid-June. Mid-Jan to mid-March used to be a period of internship at a level commensurate with the batch year.

We would try and keep in touch with Alyosha on his mobile phone, but he would not appreciate being called often and also had the propensity to lose mobile phones. Whether this was on purpose, I would not be able to say with confidence, but I suspect it was. So more often than not we would trouble his roommates to connect him to us. He had got actively involved in sports, mainly football and basketball.

Well into the second trimester, a couple of weeks before the school was to recess for the internship period, Alyosha surprised us by calling himself. He had a very peculiar and uncomfortable request. He wondered if his batch mate, Geetanjali, hailing from Jaipur and who was to intern in Delhi, could stay with us during her internship period. It was an awkward decision to make personally for both me and my wife, and while we were enlightened enough to agree, I could not have made a final call without first having spoken to her parents. Her father was a secretary level IAS officer with the Rajasthan government. We invited her parents to our house in Delhi and sought their concurrence for their daughter to stay with us during her internship. Having met us, they agreed.

It was during their internship period that I could gauge that both Geetanjali and Alyosha were keen on each other. I was neither surprised nor taken aback at such a development. It was part of a natural process of growing up. I did have a word with Alyosha, to impress upon him that while life would take its course, his primary aim was to graduate with a law degree and nothing was to deviate his focus from that. He understood the same. In more ways than one, he was beyond his years. The first year went past quickly and it seemed that Alyosha had got into the groove of life at law school.

The second year was more turbulent. He would get into some not-so pleasant situations with some of the faculty members and in particular with the Dean of Students, Ms Elizabeth. She was a spinster and showed herself a very strict and no-nonsense lady. When Alyosha got repeats in some courses, I asked him as to what he was up to. With his intellect and grasp, it was very unusual for such a development. He told me that no matter what he wrote and how he answered, he would get repeats in some classes, because he had not endeared himself to those teachers.

As I learnt, most of their discomfort stemmed from his independent streak and his conviction to state, without fear or favour, his opinion on a subject. This was irksome to some of his teachers, and being human they would react in their assessments of his assignments. This is a common failing with most of us – we do not know how to handle a subordinate or a student, who doesn't abide by conventional wisdom or taboos, but exerts his independent opinion rather freely. Such students need to be handled very carefully and with maturity so as not to hinder their questioning spirit and curiosity. A confrontational attitude could leave permanent scars. Not even for a moment is one advocating tolerance of indisciplined behavior but a teacher needs to discern dissent from disorder and treat the situation accordingly.

This reminds me of an occasion in April 2004, just a month prior to my retirement from the Navy. I had made a farewell trip to Bharat Electronic Ltd (BEL) with which I had a lot of professional dealings. During that trip, I took an afternoon off to surprise Alyosha at the Law School. I had planned to take him and his friend Satyajit out for lunch, so I reached the school just when their classes got over.

When I met Alyosha, he informed me that Ms Elizabeth wished to see me. I told him that even he hadn't known that I was to be there, so how could she be expecting me?. He said "Now that you are here, you might as well meet her". So I had this encounter with Ms Elizabeth or Lizzy as the students would call her. As soon as I entered her office and introduced myself, she took off on how Alyosha had called her a dictator in the class or words to that effect, and also how she ought to have the patience to learn even from a five year old. In the manner that she talked to me, I felt it was not talking with me but talking down to me. My years in the Navy and in command of submarines, ships and major establishments had taught me to be patient in such situations. So I heard all that she had to say and then suggested to her with respect that what Alyosha was trying to convey to her was not wrong in principle, but maybe the manner in which he had put it across could have been better.

I immediately offered an apology on his behalf and said that being a good Christian, she should forgive him. Her response left me dumbstruck. She said "I am not Jesus Christ". Having said that she also wanted to excuse herself saying she had a faculty meeting to attend. I gently reminded her that it was she who had sought to meet me and not the other way round. Before leaving, I told her that I would counsel Alyosha and that she should let the matter rest there. To my utter disappointment, that was not to be and she, as long as she remained "Dean of the Undergraduates", continued to pick on him. To my mind this was very unfortunate and reflected her immaturity. A few years after Alyosha's death, my wife and I met her on the New Year's Eve of 2012 and on the penultimate day of college, and had a long chat with her. In fact we drove with her to town and in a manner it was a catharsis for her. She finally did say that she had misunderstood him, but alas it was too late. As for Alyosha, he had forgiven her and held no grudges, something he told me in January 2007, when he had visited me in Moscow.

I have brought out this episode not with a view to run down anyone, but to highlight the importance of genuine understanding between a student and a teacher, particularly in a residential institution. In the Navy, we say: "There are no bad officers, only bad Commanding Officers". This is to imply that handling an errant officer to bring out the best in him is incumbent on the Commanding Officer. This should be the case in any didactic relationship and becomes all the more important with indigo children such as Alyosha.

It was because of this fraught relationship with Lizzy that Alyosha had a not so happy stay in Law School. By his fourth year she had ceased to be the Dean of the Undergraduates, but enough mistrust had been generated. But later, he told me that he held no rancour or ill will towards her.

Here, I must talk about the general deterioration in the manner in which the country's premier law school was being administered. I have touched upon the fact that neither the Director nor the Registrar were residing on campus, although there were houses earmarked for them. To my mind this was a major reason for the slackness in discipline.

In one of my interactions with the Director Mr Jay Govind, where Alyosha's local guardian and my colleague the late Commander Bopaiya was also present, the Director admitted to us that no one listens to him. He had banned smoking on campus, but the result of this was that students would go outside the gates and smoke and get into unpleasant altercations with the local populace, who were inherently hostile to these members of the English-speaking elite.

This coming from the Director was very strange, and both I and Commander Bopaiya felt that he lacked the administrative skills to run an institute like that. He may have been a brilliant professor but managing an institution is another matter altogether. We did suggest various measures such as designating smoking areas, as banning didn't seem to be the answer. We also suggested opening up cafeterias on campus that would remain open till late, so that students working on assignments in the library had a place to eat and didn't have to go out late at night, because they had no choice, and be unnecessarily exposed to potentially unpleasant situations with the locals.

We also suggested he put in place a robust counselling system. Most students joined NLS immediately after school and were not yet prepared to independently handle certain situations. Apparently, not much was done during his tenure to improve the situation. A few students committed suicide during this time, which perhaps could have been avoided if the situations had been monitored and handled with sympathy.

After Alyosha's passing away, I was invited by the President Bar Council of India (BCI), whose Trust used to manage the National Law School of India University, Bangalore. The Chief Justice of India was its Ex-Officio Chancellor. He candidly told me that the BCI was not satisfied with the manner in which the school was being run and had sought suggestions from me based on my experience in the Navy. I had given him a host of recommendations in writing. Subsequently, as I learnt that a committee had been set up to remedy the situation with the new Vice Chancellor taking over in end 2008. It seems that much has been done since then and the situation has improved a great deal.

Anyone who has seen the movie 3 Idiots, with Aamir Khan in the lead role will easily understand what I mean. The fact that I did not receive any official communication from the school informing me of the emergency that arose that night of Alyosha's tragic death – or subsequently – speaks volumes about the inefficiency of the administration under Mr Jay Gobind. He was a simple person but in my opinion unfit to be the Director (Vice Chancellor) of such a prestigious institution.

In Alyosha's final year in October 2006, I received a communication from the college to present myself before the college authorities to deal with a serious situation in which it was stated that some marijuana was found on his bed. Though the incident had occurred in July, the report was ready only in October 2006 after the due process had been followed. I spoke to Alyosha on the phone as I was in Moscow, and he explained to me that on that particular evening he had gone for a basketball match and injured his finger. He had gone straight to the hospital to get it attended to. By the time he got back, it was rather late and some of his friends had smoked pot there. He swore that on that evening he had nothing to do with it. I do not for a moment suggest that he would never have indulged in it. All of us have tried it in our youth. However on that particular day he had not. Someone from the student discipline body checked his room and Alyosha let them do their job. When I told him that I could take this as his defence with the Director, he said "How will it help? Someone else will get suspended, so let it be me". This showed his character of showing solidarity with his friends. Very few would act like that.

My wife flew down to Bangalore and met Alyosha's local guardian. The Discipline Committee wanted to suspend Alyosha for two terms, which would in effect mean a loss of a year. My wife pleaded with the Director that given the circumstances, a more humane view could be taken, and also that he had been preparing for his CAT for the IIMs, which would be jeopardized. The suspension was reduced to one term, which meant the loss of the Oct–Jan trimester, which he would have to do from Jul–Sep the following year. I thought that it was a fair decision, given the fact that Alyosha had wanted to take the onus upon himself. So he had to spend those three months at home in Pune, out of which he chose to come down for New Year's Eve in 2007 to Moscow to spend 10 days with me. Looking back, we feel it was destiny which enabled him to spend that time with us, as once he joined back in March 2007, we did not get to see him much. While he was at home during this trimester on forced leave, we did get him checked at a rehab centre in Pune to see if he indeed had a problem. Their finding was that he was perfectly fine.

In middle of April 2007, I visited him for three days. I found him to be really considerate and noticed that he went out of his way to make me comfortable. Usually, I would stay in town with Cdr Bopaiya but during this visit, they were away to Coorg and therefore I had to stay in Nagarbhavi. Alyosha made all the arrangements for me. This was a new side of him that showed itself, reflecting his attitude of taking more responsibility. I was very pleased. The three days spent with him were pure bliss. He even took me for a movie The Namesake on the penultimate evening. The movie is based on the novel by Jhumpa Lahiri and is directed by Mira Nair. In the novel, towards the end, Gogol reads the book in the train given to him by his father on his graduation, who has suddenly passed away due to a heart attack. The book is written by the Russian author Gogol (after whom the protagonist in the film is named, hence 'the namesake'). The movie was really interesting and somehow gave me a sense of foreboding. I could not put a finger on why but that is how it was. In hindsight, I wonder if there was a message that it would be our last meeting as I never saw him alive again.

In July the same year, my wife also flew down to Bangalore to be with him. He came to receive her at the airport, dressed in pyjamas and a kurta, looking really scruffy. She told him so and he replied "I have been looking forward to your visit with great anticipation and on seeing me all you can do is comment on my clothes". This was typical of Alyosha, but in essence he was expressing his deeply felt affection and love for his mother. In those three days, he really pampered her, even taking her to an exclusive dinner with a special menu of wine and seafood and insisted on footing the bill himself. His mother was so surprised because this was not the usual Alyosha. We cannot say, but maybe he foresaw his own fate and wanted to make it memorable for both his parents who met him separately so that their final memories of seeing him would be unforgettable.

His last examination was on 25 September 2007, which he completed successfully. An assignment that was to be submitted was recovered from his laptop and submitted. He had thus graduated to become a lawyer from the most prestigious law school in the country, despite having undergone a lot of trials and tribulations. He told me that it was his will and inner strength that enabled him to get through all that and that anyone else in his place may have given up.

We collected his degree posthumously in the convocation held in August 2008. Although it had no practical value, I still looked at it as the fruit of his labours. In his memory we instituted a gold medal at NLS for the best student in sports and extracurricular activities. He himself had been sportsman of the year from 2005-2007. The students Bar Association has also named their common room in his memory. It is their tribute to him.

~ 14 ~

Corruption & Our Youth

The story of corruption in Indian public life is an old one. Yet, there was distinct break in this narrative in 2011, thanks to a septuagenarian in the avatar of Shri Anna Hazare who led an important, if ultimately short-lived, anti-corruption movement. While he was its leader, it was the youth of India that really gave it its strength and energy – so powerful that it forced our Parliament to rise above partisanship and accede to the will of the people. Four years later, Narendra Modi and the BJP party also won the national election on an anti-corruption platform.

Alyosha too was a very honest and fastidious person, who would not tolerate injustice and got really agitated when faced with corruption. Two incidents come to mind. The first relates to his getting a driving licence. He turned 18 in December 2002, becoming eligible for a driving licence. I was still in the Navy then and posted at Naval HQ as a Commodore and in a position of some influence. We were living in Sangli Officer's Apartments on Copernicus Marg in Delhi. I used to go for my daily morning run to Lodhi Gardens and there I made friends with the vehicle licensing inspector of the New Delhi zone, who too was a regular walker.

So, in January 2003, when Alyosha was doing his first year internship as part of the NLS curriculum, I arranged for him to get a driving licence. The process starts with a learner's licence and only after a minimum period of one month of learning, can one give the road test for a permanent licence. I suggested to Alyosha that I could, using my influence with the Inspector, get that period waived off as a special case. However, Alyosha would have nothing to do with it. He insisted on going through the laid down procedure.

Sometime at the end of February, he went for his road test. I had mentioned this to the inspector in my morning walk that day, who directed the examiner to take an abbreviated test. However, Alyosha refused to be accorded special dispensation and underwent the complete test successfully. I know that one can obtain a driving licence, even without visiting a licencing office, by going through touts or agents. But Alyosha would never have agreed to take recourse to such a route.

It so happened that within a year his wallet got picked along with his licence. When his mother took him to the same licensing office to get a duplicate (by which time I had left the Navy), the clerk tried troubling them, obviously looking for a bribe. Alyosha got agitated and his mother had to calm him down. The duplicate was eventually issued, after the intervention of the same inspector, who was still there.

The second incident occurred in May 2007. Alyosha's batch at NLS had organized a party prior to graduation. Someone from the catering staff managed to pick the pockets of some of the boys at that get-together, including Alyosha's, with his debit card in it. The next day the card had been used for shopping worth Rs 18,000/-. HDFC bank wanted a FIR to be lodged before investigating the misuse of the debit card.

Alyosha with his roommate, whose father was a DGP and the second most senior police officer in Karnataka, went to the police station to lodge a FIR. He had already cautioned his friend that they would have a problem doing so as the sub-inspector on duty would demand a bribe. He was proved right, but both of them kept on arguing with him. They indicated that they were law students and hence knew the law, and countered all the excuses the sub inspector gave to prevent them from filing a FIR. After spending six hours in vain, Alyosha and his friend went out and rang up the friend's father, who advised them to wait till he spoke to the station house officer. He then rang them back and asked them to approach the SI again. This time the SI was most apologetic and went out of his way to be nice, and registered the FIR.

That should have been the end of the matter, but Alyosha told him that he also wanted to file a complaint against him for dereliction of duty. This he did. As a result, the SI got suspended and the entire incident was covered by a local news daily. It was this fastidiousness in Alyosha that is widely reflected in today's youth. Alyosha chose law as his profession in order to fight for the rights of the disempowered and the marginalized. He wanted to do social litigation. Overall, I believe this young generation is not as cynical as people of mine were; they feel assured that they can bring about a change in the systemic institutions of this country. Rest in Peace Alyosha. The values you lived for were not in vain.

The Trial

The Immediate Aftermath

"They've been nabbed by the cops," said Commander Mathur, my ex-colleague from the Navy, as soon as I exited the airport at Bangalore, having arrived from Moscow as soon as I'd heard the news. He meant the two urchins behind Alyosha's murder. I felt a bit odd because through the journey I had I only reflected on Alyosha's life from the time he was born on that freezing afternoon of December 1984 in Vladivostok. When I heard this, it dawned on me that the trial would have to be dealt with and at that precise moment, I had no idea as to how. The first task however was to get Alyosha's body released from the police custody and complete the cremation.

I had arrived in the wee hours of 1 October 2007, and after catching a few winks, which were hard to come by, my wife and I were taken to the mortuary in the forenoon to formally identify the body. It was heartbreaking for us, to say the least, to see Alyosha's slain body. It had eleven stab wounds though only one proved fatal. The post mortem was to be done only after that. A brief statement was taken from me by the Investigating Officer.

The body was released after the post mortem an hour later and we were able to proceed to the crematorium just an hour after noon. The cremation had been completed by about 4pm. It was only after we had returned to the rest house from the crematorium, that our thoughts turned to the issue of the investigation into the incident.

I may add that prior to reaching Bangalore, while I was waiting at Frankfurt Airport for a connecting flight, I had informed my ex-colleague Mr KP Singh from the Ministry of Defence, who was then a Secretary in the Home Ministry, in charge of border security, about what had happened. I had also informed Mr Dhirendra Singh, who I had worked with in the Ministry of Defence, whilst steering the Scorpene submarine programme, and who had retired as the Home Secretary to the Government of India. Both these accomplished gentlemen were from the Karnataka cadre of the IAS.

In the afternoon, after the cremation, I received a call from Mr KP Singh informing me that he had spoken to the DG police of Karnataka, who would get in touch with me. Sure enough I got a call from him a little later. Speaking to him, I only made one request – that he appoint a competent investigating officer, who should conduct his investigation in a thorough and professional manner, and which would stand scrutiny in the court during the trial. In my experience of such issues, more often than not, the police bungle the initial investigation and as a result the case fails in the courts. The DGP assured me that he would ensure that one of his best IOs with an able assisting team would handle the case.

The next day 2 October, we had gone to Srirangapatnam, where the sangam of the three holy rivers in the South namely; Cauvery, (Kaveri), Kabini, and Hemavati takes palace. It is considered to be a holy spot for the immersion of the ashes of a departed soul. I also knew that Alyosha was very fond of this place as he had written to me about having driven down there a few times and had found the solitude and peace he experienced there very uplifting. So it was but natural that a portion of his remains were immersed there and the remaining in Hardwar a couple of days later.

On the 3rd of October, we visited NLS and interacted with the Vice Chancellor, some faculty members, who were well-disposed towards Alyosha and some of his friends. They were all distraught at what had happened. The VC informed us that the alumni association had decided to appoint a lawyer to fight the case alongside the State. This was a very welcome and good gesture from the alumni association and took a lot of load off my chest. I had been reflecting on this aspect and had been wondering how I could ensure proper conduct of the prosecution's case, as we were not residents of Bangalore. A close monitoring is most essential to ensure a conviction, even though it was almost inevitable in this case, since there were five eye witnesses, who were all Alyosha's friends from law school.

The case may have appeared to be an open-and-shut one, but it still had to be proved in court. For this, thorough investigations needed to be conducted to build a watertight case. The conduct of the case by the Prosecution in the court was also most essential. With the assurance from the DGP on the investigation, the offer of the Alumni to appoint a lawyer to assist the prosecutor and in acting as an interface between the police, prosecutor and us, a major step towards ensuring delivery of justice had been taken. In this regard, I must make a mention of the-then President of the NLSIU Alumni Association Aditya Bhat and his colleague CK Nanda Kumar, who though years senior to Alyosha, were very helpful and personally kept me informed on the developments in the initial phase of the investigation. My wife and I owe them an eternal debt of gratitude.

Although the two accused of committing the actual murder and the auto driver had been apprehended, the four guys in the Sumo, who had initiated the altercation, were absconding. They were finally caught in Mysore ten days later. Three of them had shaved of their heads to change their appearance. All six were remanded to police custody to enable the investigation. The way the investigation progressed reassured me that the DGP had been true to his word. The investigating officer was a very competent police inspector and was overseeing the investigation thoroughly.

The advocate appointed by the alumni association was Mr Y Nagaraj, an ex-inspector of police himself, who had kindly agreed to assist. He was to be my main contact person during the investigation and the conduct of the trial. I found him to be competent, intelligent, conscientious and thoroughly committed to the task at hand. I would not be wrong to say that his contribution in securing a conviction was crucial. He also conducted his brief without any serious consideration for a high remuneration. He wanted the ends of justice met in this case for justice's own sake.

The appointment of a competent prosecutor to conduct the case was still an issue that was worrying me. I had sufficient background in law, being the son of a constitutional expert and also having been associated with a few Courts ¬ Martial in the navy, as a Defence Counsel as also as the President of the Court, to understand the importance of a competent prosecution.

At that time, Karnataka had a BJP government headed by Mr Yedurappa as the Chief Minister. I took the liberty of writing to Mr Arun

Jaitely, then a member of the Rajya Sabha and General Secretary of the party to use his good offices with the State Government to appoint a competent public prosecutor to execute the prosecution's case. I must acknowledge that Mr Jaitely responded with alacrity and sensitivity and promptly forwarded my request to the Chief Minister.

I have highlighted these aspects only to emphasize that getting justice in criminal cases in particular for a common person in our system, is not easy. In my case, given the position I enjoyed as a senior retired naval officer, and having access to people in the executive, did play a role. I did not seek favours but only implored that the system work as it should, because often, due to its apathy, it fails to deliver. My wife and I had consciously decided that we would not associate ourselves with the day-to-day hearings in the case as that would cause continuous emotional stress. I had seen how the lives of many families in similar cases had been scarred for life.

Having done my bit to see that the investigation and the prosecution would progress diligently, I could feel reassured. However, the wheels of justice in our great country do not move with the speed at which they should. Although the initial investigation was done with professionalism and the chargesheet filed within the stipulated period of 90 days, the case thereafter did not move, having been committed to the session court by the Chief Metropolitan Magistrate. The gang of four had also managed to obtain bail for themselves since they were not directly charged for murder under Section 302 of the Indian Penal Code. However, the two principal accused did not get bail being accused of murder. The hearings in the case would keep getting adjourned under one pretext or another. Sometimes the Judge, a lady, would herself not turn up on account of ill health, feigned or otherwise I can't say. All these developments would cause frustration and I would at times tend to take them out on Mr Nagaraj, who always kept me informed, and advocated patience on our part. Thus the trial meandered along till the summer of 2008.

In August 2008, my wife and I had gone to attend the convocation of the NLSIU where we had to collect Alyosha's BA, LLB degree. I was specially called out at the last to receive the parchment from the Chief Justice of India, Justice KG Balakrishnan, who was the Ex-Officio Chancellor of NLS. It was a very poignant moment for me. The fruits of Alyosha's labour were reduced symbolically to that parchment, and regrettably he would not be around to practice his profession, which he had so dearly aspired in order to uplift the underprivileged.

The Breakthrough
Just after the convocation ceremony whilst

we were still seated, a gentleman named Aditya Sondhi approached me. He was a 1998 batch alumnus of the law school and was running his own law firm in Bangalore. Of his own accord he offered me his services to help monitor the trial and to offer advice as and when needed. This was totally unexpected, but the help was welcome.

It reinforced my belief in the goodness of human beings. He nominated two of his juniors, Nidhishree Venugopal in the initial stages and Guru in the later stages. They would give me feedback independent of Mr Nagaraj. With so much support, one never felt the need to attend the hearings. Our original decision was vindicated and we could go about rebuilding our lives instead of having to relive the tragedy in the court at every hearing. I owe much gratitude to Aditya Sondhi, in particular, because he did all of this gratis, despite my offering him remuneration.

During the better part of 2008, the trial seemed stuck and was not progressing. In October that year, I was constrained and frustrated enough to write to Justice Balakrishnan, the Chief Justice of India, more so since he was the Ex-Officio Chancellor of the NLSIU and a student of his University had been brutally murdered. I informed him that the eyewitness students would pass out of the law school in 2009 and go for higher studies, possibly even abroad. To get them as witnesses then would be extremely difficult, if not impossible. Hence it was imperative that their testimonies were completed. I am sure he must have issued directions to the Karnataka High Court to ensure that the trial got a move on. I may add that the case had been assigned to Fast Track Court No 1. After my letter to the CJI in October 2008, there was a discernible movement forward. A new no-nonsense Judge was appointed in early 2009, who remained till the conclusion of the trial.

My wife did attend some hearings but soon realized the futility of it, because in one instance, upon reaching the court, it was learnt that the hearing had been adjourned to a later date without the court even sitting. At such times, one obviously felt very frustrated but patience was the only virtue in such circumstances. The biggest and most sustained support during the trial came from our dearest friend and colleague from the Navy, Cdr Manda Bopaiya and his wife Sumathi, who were always there for us throughout those trying times. Many a times he would go on his own to attend the hearings. Another friend Cmde (Retd) PP Singh and his wife Poonam were also present in Bangalore to give support. Between PP & Manda, they ensured that no hearing was ever missed. It is this kind of unconditional support that sustained and carried us through. Cdr Bopaiya, unfortunately is no more having himself departed on his last journey in February 2013. Without him as a pillar of strength, we would have found it extremely difficult.

The End of the Trial

The trial progressed much faster in 2009 and 2010, and one hoped for its conclusion by end 2010 or early 2011. But a roadblock emerged June 2010 onwards. A number of police witnesses, who were involved at some stage of the investigation, would not produce themselves for their deposition. Either they were on bandobast duties – for example, soon after the Allahabad High Court delivered its verdict on Ayodhya in September 2010 or assigned to some other task. Once again I had to write to the DGP, Karnataka, to request him to ensure that the police witnesses were spared and produced in court for their depositions. A nudge from Mr Dhirendra Singh, also helped. As a result, all the police witnesses, whose testimonies were a formality, were produced on two consecutive days. I, once again, wish to emphasize that if one takes it up with the appropriate authority in writing, some good does come out of it.

The leading of evidence and cross-examinations were completed by the middle of autumn 2011, and the arguments of the prosecution and the defence concluded by October 2011. The judgement was expected by end December. However, the Judge's steno fell sick and the judgement got further delayed. It was then slated for 20 February, 2012, but once again could not be pronounced as one of the accused had got into a fight in Bangalore jail and had been transferred to Belgaum, and hence could not be produced in court. The judge took a very serious view and directed the SHO of the Police Station in the case, Jnan Bharti, to send an inspector with an escort to bring the accused to the court by 12pm on 22 February for the final judgment.

So on the 22nd February, all the accused were assembled in the court by 2pm and the judgment was read out. Accused 1 and 2 were convicted for murder under Section 302 of the IPC. Accused 3 to 6 (the Sumo gang) were acquitted as the charge of criminal conspiracy could not be proved. It was ironic because the incident had been initiated by them. The convicted felons were awarded life imprisonment.

In a sense four years, four months and four weeks after the incident, the trial came to its conclusion, bringing closure to us. However, I feel that when you lose your only child closure never comes; one just has to cope with it. I had been keen to see the ends of justice were met for the sake of justice itself. Criminal elements floating in society must know and understand that the long arm of the law will catch up with them sooner or later.

During one of our visits to Bangalore to meet Mr Nagaraj and the public prosecutor while the trial was still on, the constable who would accompany accused no 1 and 2 to court came up to my wife and I and said: "Sir, I am convinced that in this case justice will be done, because all the witnesses have been coming. In my more than 20 years of service, I have not seen this happen. Mostly witnesses do not turn up. In such a scenario, how does one expect the judge to arrive at a verdict?" We were very relieved to hear that, but his observations speak eloquently about the deficiencies in our criminal justice system. Another aspect is that witnesses are either bought or threatened. Even the advocates of one party are compromised by the other side by lure or by inducements. All I can say from my experience in this trial is that one has to persevere and not give up.

The present day media plays a significant role in highlighting the plight of the underdog in securing justice. However, my own view is that whilst the media may help, it should refrain from sensationalism for the sake of TRPs. Their job should be to bring out the helplessness and plight of the litigants in situations where the wheels of justice are not moving. Most of the time, in trying to sensationalise news, the media can actually harm the case.

Another aspect is the tactics the defence employs in delaying the trial on frivolous grounds. In most cases, the judges indulge them by giving adjournments. It happened in this case as well, particularly in the initial stages. However, we were fortunate with the replacement judge who came later and was a tough cookie. He never allowed delaying tactics and at times told the defence that he would impose fines/costs on them if a prosecution witness who was on the stand had to be called again for cross examination on frivolous grounds. Diligence and firmness in conducting the trial is essential to the timely delivery of justice.

In the end, I would say that we were blessed and fortunate to have seen through the trial without ever being integral to its proceedings. We had a strong support system of friends and well-wishers, who saw the trial to its conclusion. We were allowed to rebuild our lives and cope with the grief in the best manner possible.

~ *16* ~

Afterword

Alyosha lived for exactly 22 years, 10 months and 20 days. It was a short life in contemporary measure. A life cut short by the cruel hands of fate. Had he lived on, I have no doubt that he would have influenced society around him in a positive manner. It was, alas, not to be. However, even in his short life, there are many facets of his character which came to the fore and which can serve as an example to the younger generation.

So what is it that one must remember Alyosha by? I feel that his life epitomized the fact that one must live adhering steadfastly to one's convictions, without compromising one's beliefs, with complete honesty and with compassion to one's fellow beings. His unflinching honesty was also rare and admirable. As his roommate during his initial years in law school and his very close friend Arun Srikumar said of him: "I can tell you honestly, that he (Alyosha) is the only person I know, who has never, to my knowledge, spoken an untruth. He was boldly honest, even if it meant getting into trouble. For that alone, he won the love and admiration of every person he met. The other thing that I will always remember about him is that he never ever meant anyone any harm. It was really rare in our community to see someone with absolutely no malice towards even a single person. When he had disagreements with another's point of view (especially faculty, who were all half crazy!!), he would try to reason things out and appeal to their sense of rationality, which was truly remarkable."

Other facets of his personality were evident in his conduct throughout his short life, but in the last moments before his tragic death, his courage to defend the honour of his friend, wherein most would have fled, shone above everything else. One of his fellow students in the Law School, musing on some of the suicides and deaths in the National Law School, wrote:

"The most painful was, of course, Alyosha's murder. Speaking to an ex-NLSIU faculty member, I came to know that Alyosha's murder was sought to be explained away by some drug deal gone wrong. That Alyosha, who had been ratted out to the faculty (for possessing ganja, and how many SC advocates from Law faculty or other colleges haven't?), was some sort of mafia member. I got so angry that the professor back tracked. "They probably wanted the girl," he mused.

I thought about it quite long and hard and one evening it all came to me. If those guys were willing to stab a guy in order to kidnap a girl, imagine what they would have done to her if they had succeeded. No person with a shred of conscience would ever allow that to happen to one of his friends. Yet in moments of blind panic, people are selfish.

My first New Year's Eve in Bangalore, we walking back to campus around 1am, and a group of six or seven guys on three bikes rode past, shouting obscenities at the girls walking with us . 'Fuck you, I shouted back, and then 'Oh fuck', as they turned around and came back at us. Almost every one fled, leaving a girl, a Sri Lankan, behind. Two of the bikers grabbed her arms from each side as if trying to rip her into two. The one or two who did not run made a big difference that evening.

Alyosha Kumar, an ex-army school kid, never taking bull crap from anyone, died the way he lived. A Hero. So now I don't feel so bad anymore. He did the right thing and took one for the team. There are better things than living a long life, no matter how accomplished, as a coward. The truth is our society, especially university professors, do not have the depth to recognize true acts of courage and bravery."
Shakespeare in his play Julius Caesar says:

> *"Cowards die many times before their deaths.*
> *The valiant never taste of death but once.*
> *Of all the wonders that I yet have heard,*
> *It seems to me most strange that men should fear,*
> *Seeing that death, a necessary end,*

Will come when it will come."

So Alyosha died displaying his daring and courage, of which he himself was so proud. To his parents in particular and to those who knew him in general, his loss has been monumental. The solace lies in the fact that even though short, Alyosha lived his life to the full, the way he wanted to and on his own terms. Not many can say that about their lives. In the end, we need to celebrate his short time with us, like that of a bright shooting star, and not mourn his tragic death.

~ 16 ~

Emails – Son to Father

Dearest Papa,
Things are somewhat relaxed in college now that most of everyone's formalities are done. I do not feel any different. I still have the hunger and curiosity for knowledge that I had before. If anything, the prospect of leaving has got my learning and interest juices going like an enthusiastic schoolkid.
Intend to visit the Bopaiyas and Poonam aunty sometime soon.

Tuesday, May 8, 2007 11:46 AM
(After one his last exams.)

There was the usual revelry but I can enjoy other people's pleasure without becoming completely caught up in it myself and I suppose that is what I did. I was quite careful and the whole convocation week was quite event free. Hope you people are doing great.. Send me picture of your time in Mexico and the United States.
Friday, August 24, 2007 11:22 PM
(On farewell bash of his batch in May '07)

Dearest Papa,

With the kind of logical brain and good reasoning I know you possess, your advice about the North-East would sound like tripe to even you. I do not know how it could jeopardise my completing college. No more anyway than it would jeopardise my life if I went as a graduate. The only extra factor you mention is my luck, which I must admit is difficult to factor in because it is so volatile.

Send me Sumathi aunty and Manda uncle's cell numbers. For some reason their landline number seems to have changed within the last month. Went with my last wallet. Also am attaching mama's cardholder dispute form in full. Ask her to fill it as it is. Also ask her to send a handwritten letter of authorisation saying her card was with me, and that I can carry out the procedures in pursuance of an insurance dispute. What is happening with your insurance dispute?

The car's alternator has gone again and the keys are in Goa so I have to get the Maruti people to take it to the service station. Take care.

Tuesday, June 12, 2007
(On his desire to go to NE in summer of '07 and my suggestion to defer it till after graduation.)

What is most distressing is your making not getting a call every 3 days such a pain for me that it is suffocating. Slipping on my word what are you saying?? I have spoken at least twice a week to you and every saturday but yesterday. Stop letting mama get to you, when you know I would call you if I were making any plans, despite how useless and unconstructive you would be. I had a repeat exam Friday that did not go so great.. IF she is inclined to pass rather than fail people, I should pass so keep your fingers crossed...

If not then it is down the barrel of another year, so...

I have another repeat exam wednesday so I think my plans of going anywhere are quite put paid to... This one I have been compelled to do by default, for a 20-mark question on two movies which were screened while I had other classes to attend. Teacher says no alternate evaluation can be provided, "just write the repeat"..

Life as ever is livable but horrible around college. take care and I will call you...

Sunday, June 24, 2007

Dearest Papa,
I had an eye-opening interview with HLL on Friday. eye-opening because of how blatantly you are a 'commodity' at times, like was thecase in the interview. Anyhow, I am applying to anything and everything whether or not I am going to get it. In class so have to keep it short.

Tuesday, April 24, 2007

~ 18 ~

Emails – From Alyosha's Friends

A letter I had promised long back

Dear Mr and Mrs. Kumar,

I had told you of these scribbled notes last year during the funeral. I had wanted to meet you when you had come for the convocation, but something kept me back. It is a bit difficult for me to talk about him, or to face you. I only manage to do so with a small group of close friends who knew him as well as I did. But, still, I finally thought that I should at least mail you.

These are notes that Alyosha scribbled on some note paper in my room when he came to talk to me, but I was half asleep. So he wrote on three small note sheets, back and front, and left, saying he'd come by in the morning. I woke up later at night, and was touched by what he had written. To provide some context, this was when we had both lost years due to DPC. The parts in [ ] are my additions.

"Dearest Pranesh, This is the first letter I have written to a boy that's like this, and that is definitely not an unmitigated compliment. You inspire this extraordinary tenderness in me. So you failed. So I failed. Prashansa Poddar (dunno why) Kranti (the chick CR), Parashar, Vedula, Parag Sayta, Arjun Ghosh are some of the people I think I could get to know better. By the end of that year, the prospects in that list will be different. But that's the whole point. Life panning out, regardless of the best laid plans, the rigorous schemes. Come to think of it, our lives are already more interesting than the Gitanjalis [he's scratched this out, but one can make out -PP] Jagannaths and Ramyas of the world, only because we have failed a year, nothing else. It's an experience I know Gitanjali has missed out on.

The excruciating waiting to know, the rush of a Shankara repeat and of course the relief of knowing you have failed (or passed). Didn't you just want out of your [smudged word] 3rd yr so bad by the end? We can even enjoy knowing laughs when (hope not or pretend to haha) when Satyajit joins us. We timed it well. No special repeat, no pain. Moderate the panning out with your efforts, but cherish, preserve yourself. Sleep your snoring self well, honeypie, for you'll only know my fond wish in the morn. Love, Alyosha. P.S.: A tiny pat on the 'tush' and a kiss on the head will have to suffice for now. [In a small box:] Let's do [unclear word] in the year, part-time. [In a small box:] 2 polos [that he had taken from my table]"

I condole with you in your loss. It is almost as great a loss for me. He was a darling chap, and a good friend. There were many things we shared, and many things we disagreed about. Many were the times I was confounded by him -- his complete lack of "property" (he would treat everyone's as his, and would allow everyone to treat his as theirs), for instance. All that I have of him now are these notes, a sweater, and memories. I wished to share some of them with you.

Much love,
Pranesh Prakash
Wednesday, October 1, 2008 10:31 PM

Dear uncle,

Many thanks for your email and for your blessing for our project. I am happy to share with you that we have already collected in excess of the budgeted expenditure for the proposed inaugural Alyosha Kumar Memorial Football Tournament at NLS, which will be held in the 4th week of August. I will let you know what continued progress we make on that front, and keep you posted on the exact dates of that event as well. You can rest assured we will keep this effort alive for many many years to come.

I am also extremely delighted that you have set up the Brave New World trust in Al's memory. I am quite sure that many of us who had the pleasure and joy of studying and interacting with Al will get involved in some way or other with the wonderful things you intend to do with this effort to keep his spirit alive. I will circulate your appeal note among our batchmates and also among his friends and well-wishers from the law school community. I am hopeful you will see encouraging responses, which will only grow in the years to come.

It was immensely moving to read Al's handwritten note, which once again shows maturity far beyond his years (which he demonstrated even to the very end). You are 120% right when you say that he stood by what he believed and that he was a soul of rare courage. I can tell you honestly that he is the ONLY person I know who has never to my knowledge spoken an untruth. He was boldly honest, even if it meant it got him in trouble. For that alone, he won the love and admiration of every person he met. The other thing that I will always recall about him is that he never EVER meant anyone any harm. It was really rare in our community to see someone with absolutely no malice toward even a single person. Even where he had disagreements with others' points of view (especially faculty, who were all half crazy!!), he would always try to reason things out and appeal to their sense of rationality, which was truly, truly remarkable.

I am very very sure we will all get to meet him someday, if we are lucky. I was with him only a few hours before the tragedy, when we met quite by coincidence at the cricket stadium. He was extremely chirpy and on top of the world in those few hours, in the knowledge that he was finishing his stint at NLS soon. I could not bear to come meet you the next day, even though I was in Bangalore. It took me many weeks to make my peace with what had happened; but I'd like you to know that he was at an incredibly happy place in his last few hours.

Al was always extremely proud about his family and of his years in Lawrence School; I am sure he will be so happy to see that you and his schoolmaster are both involved in keeping his dreams alive. This is very inspirational for all of us.

On a final note, yes, my dad is now in the hot seat in Karnataka. I will get him to put the requisite word through to the prosecution team to ensure things go ok in terms of opposing bail for accused 1 and 2. Please do let me know what happens at the trial, as and when you are informed by your sources -and also do not hesitate to let me know as and when you think any addl effort needs to be made from the prosecution side.

Warm regards to you and Deepa aunty,
Arun Srikumar, Class of 2007 - National Law School
Wed, 30 Jul 2008

A letter for you from Nimesh - a roommate of Aly

hey Malavika
I don't know Alyosha's parents email id. please forward this mail to them...

Dear Aunt and Uncle,

I am sorry for writing late but whenever I log on, I visit Alyosha's blog and read it again and again; almost everyday I read the mails we wrote to each other, and so many times I have read the testimonial he wrote for me in orkut. I don't know whether Alyosha ever talked about me, but I am someone who counted Alyosha among one of the closest, most lovable and valuable persons in his life. I was his roommate for one year in law school (in 2005-6) and I really loved Alyosha like my younger brother. We shared great affinity for each other and felt very comfortable in each others company. We used to talk to each others for hours on phone after I left Bangalore. We regularly wrote mail to each other. I remember our last long talk; Alyosha telling me how eagerly he is waiting to start afresh in Mumbai, we making an inchoate plan for small tour around Bangalore, he asking me to pray for one of his bua who was very ill at that time. I also remember me waking him up in the night (31 st August) to tell him that I got a teacher's job in a small law college and how happy I am. In fact I could not talk for long because he was very sleepy and I promised to call him soon. But that was the last talk...., but still I just keep on telling things to Alyosha in my thought though it's too sad to not have Alyosha's brotherly and ruthlessly frank opinion on those things. I just miss the honesty and innocence of his conversation.

I was not sure whether to write openly on his blog or write a personal mail. I know so far my understanding with Alyosha goes, none of these things actually matter or probably like the way I just felt Alyosha would say " Nimesh ! Man! You just can't say that these things do not matter, and I would say "no man I am not saying that these things do not matter at all but I don't think EVERYBODY can understand what I intend to say or in fact I don't know whether I would be able to say what I intend to say.... and the talk will go on...

I want to tell you Uncle that Alyosha respected you a lot and in fact he idolized you. Not because you are his father but because he believed that you are truly a great man. Believe me, Alyosha had great understanding of human character. He loved his mom a lot and always wanted to make her happy. In fact I think he was quite close to his one bua also. I think Alyosha also loved his sister a lot and I still remember him telling me with great "Alyosha's passion" that his sis has won an award for best performance in her company.

Alyosha knew that he was superior than most of the people around him and it was impossible for Alyosha to tolerate mediocrity and injustice. It was not possible for Alyosha to love or hate someone or something simply because you are supposed to love or hate them. In fact we came close to each other by simply talking about different people in law school and our opinion on them and most of the time we liked similar kind of people. I still remember Alyosha's reading me a passage from his favorite Nietzsche's book, Nietzsche was talking about the Artist of Life. Like a true Artist of life, Alyosha had to give "Color Alyosha" to everything around him, even at the cost of ridiculousness; I really don't know how many people actually saw his utter contempt for widespread mechanization of life in his ridiculousness but I am sure Alyosha influenced everybody around him; I constantly feel a small Alyosha living inside me and I am sure that he will continue putting that Color Alyosha in everything that I do, think and speak.

Alyosha loved outdoor and free thinking as well and he was always irritated by any attempt to confine him within any boundary whatsoever. Nobody could control Alyosha, this is the major reason I am reluctant to write anything but my personal experience with Alyosha and do not want to publish them for the population. Though I know Alyosha coveted popularity and actually would have been happy seeing so many people writing about him. Believe me uncle and I am not saying it just for the sake of saying it, it is impossible for me to describe how big a personal loss it is for me. These are difficult times, and we true companion of Alyosha has to do only one thing. Just to love him back as much he loved us, but no sad memory. There was nothing sad about him so any sadness because of him is intolerable. I don't think he ever wanted anything but the return of the true and free love that he believed in. Man! I really believe that we failed to love you as much and as freely as you did, but you know man I really liked you a lot.

I would love to meet both of you someday.

Take care.

Nimesh
Thursday, October 18, 2007

THANKS FOR EVERYTHING

Seldom does one meet people in life who can speak their mind with fearless integrity and back that up with a disarming smile. Society has for centuries mastered the art of indoctrinating us into saying the right things at the right times in the right way. Most of us, most of the time, struggle to say what is really on our mind for fear of hurting either the listener or ourselves and this is a function of how society has shaped us.

Yet, some amongst us have managed to break free. Some amongst us(very very few of us)have retained the independence of thought that the infancy of the human form bestows. These rare folks exhibit an extraordinary disdain for social constructs of respecting people merely on account of their stature, of being mindlessly submissive to authority, of saying what the other person wants to hear, of being what someone else wants them to be.

As a society, these are the people we fear the most, for they care not what they speak. As human beings, these are the people we love the most, for they are refreshing in their uninhibited demeanour and inspiring by their clarity of thought. Sometimes, these people are appreciated, but only when their truth works for us. At most times, they are misunderstood because our clouded vision and conditioned thinking cannot fathom their clarity of thought. But all of us, universally love these people and secretly wish to be like them, knowing fully well that we cannot!

These mavericks never have it easy and are often dubbed as being crazy or ahead of their times. The truth is the times never really change, neither does society's parochialism. The happy part though is that these people don't change either. They stand for what they believe in – through life and beyond.

Such people inspire the rest of us (howsoever briefly) to allow the mind to freefall, to not accept anything without questioning, to place reason before obeisance. Such people touch our lives in ways that we don't realize until much later.

As the news of Alyosha's tragic demise sunk in last week, I reflected on the years that I have known him and tried to figure out what exactly he meant to me. We weren't BEST FRIENDS, we seldom hung out in the same circles, we didn't exchange many secrets – yet I couldn't shrug it aside and say that he was just another guy I knew. The fact of the matter is that, in a silent, almost inconspicuous, manner, Al had endeared himself to me. I was proud to know a guy like him, I admired his fearlessness, envied his brutal honesty and genuinely admired him, without ever being able to articulate that to myself. I realised that night that he was the guy I always wanted to be but knew I never could.

Alyosha was my renaissance man – perhaps he couldn't fight the decadence that pervades Nagarbhavi – but he sure gave it a fight. In an appropriate situation (a more fortunate one) he would've been someone like Che, we will never know, but he was one of those endearing rebels, who remained relevant irrespective of the cause.

I wish I had the opportunity to say what I felt about him to him. Though to be be perfectly honest, I know I would never be able to, because I never could be like him – I could never say it as it is, not like he could. But I wish I could. I really do.

Thanks Al. Thanks for everything. I could never tell you, but you taught me so much, without ever trying to. Today I have the answer to what Alyosha was to me – not a friend, not a buddy – probably a Hero!

Tuffloo

Catcher in the Rye

On a routine flight from Ahmedabad to Delhi, I had the seat 1A thanks to the fact that our very dedicated family travel agent guarantees this seat! 1B was empty and in 1 C, was a very distinguished but troubled and irate gentleman who had no idea that this flight from Mumbai actually stopped over for a good hour in Ahmedabad! Uncle Arun had an air of being more troubled by the world than by delayed flights. The flight eventually took off and Uncle seemed to calm down visibly and settled down to several newspapers. I wondered why he seemed so troubled but it seemed a private angst and I did not like to intrude.

Neither uncle nor I used the seat between us though he did park his many mobile phones on it temporarily. I continued to read my book and must even have dozed off a little. As I began to wake from the nap, I had the strangest sense that the seat next to me was occupied. With eyes closed it is easy to imagine things and I duly woke myself up and ascertained that this was not the case. I must have nodded off again and with eyes closed, this feeling returned so I eventually woke up as we appeared to be ready to land. Uncle Arun was slightly less cross about his delay now and as we were both bored as the aircraft circled Delhi in loops, we got to talking.

I rarely chat to complete strangers and figured this was one of those random conversations about the weather and places of orgin that one has with fellow travellers. However there is such a sense of great grief and heartfelt anguish about Arun Uncle that it is very hard not to want to know what causes it. Once again, I had a sense that there was someone sitting in the seat between us or that I was somehow talking to more than one person. This was not a tangible thing – just a presence that entirely without proof but palpable. When Uncle spoke about Alyosha I found it hard not to cry myself but it was when he said how much he missed him that I realised in a flash that Alyosha is always with them both – his parents. All the time, every step of the way. It became clear to me who the presence was in the seat between us.

I think I mentioned this to uncle a few times on the bus and at baggage claim but perhaps he thought I was being polite. Uncle and I managed to hurriedly exchange contacts based on our mutual interest in education and he asked me to look up deserving students whom Alyosha's trust could sponsor. Looking up the website later that week and finally seeing Alyosha made me certain that this was the beautiful presence on the plane.

Soon, Uncle Arun and my mother who runs the Sree Vidya

Niketan Trust for Chaitanya School in Gandhinagar were corresponding regularly and we had found the fatherless Komal (a 4th Grader at Chaitanya), a wonderful benfactor. I hope one day, Komal can hear the story of Alyosha and the amazing impact he has had on her life and the inspiration he is to so many of us. Perhaps it might allow her to sense her own father and the many fond spirits that guide us from the beyond?

The Buddha extols us to 'Live as if we might die tomorrow…' Alyosha exemplifies this in his amazing foresight and awareness even as a delightful 9 year old who contemplated with great peace, charity and equanimity, his own death. Perhaps he realised the truth that so many of us are searching for – 'that there is no death, just a change of states.' And now, here he is, still around everyone he cares about, still reaching out to young children in need of a leg up and a helping hand.

I feel very blessed and privileged to have met Alyosha and Uncle Arun in this strange and wonderful manner. It is an honour, in some tiny way, to be a conduit for his wider purpose as a moving spirit in the life of his parents and these children.

Thank you Alyosha – please stick around, lots of helpless, sometimes heartbroken kids, everywhere, need you as do your parents and theirs. Be their Little Prince, the Catcher in the Rye.

Regards, love and light,
Shubha Koshy.

Sir,

It is with the deepest sincerity that I would like to take this opportunity to thank you for the Alyosha Kumar Gold Medal for sports and co-curricular activities that I was fortunate to receive this year.

I think it is ironic that I am getting this medal, because, truthfully, before I came to NLS I was, at best, a very mediocre sportsman who could barely make it to any sports team, and I have no doubt I would have continued in the same vein if I had not had the fortune of interacting with your late son. I still remember the fateful day, six years ago, as if it were yesterday. It was the second half of a basketball game in which our college was fighting an uphill battle to retain some semblance of respect after being wholly outplayed and outmatched by the other team in the first half. However, then came Alyosha into the game. When he was called in to play by the captain, he didn't seem happy or sad or nervous as anyone would be, but instead, he was furious and screamed, " Why are you so scared of them that none of you are even playing your normal game? They aren't better than you- WE can win – just stop playing like whimps and grow a pair! ", and after that he threw himself into the game with all the gusto and fervour that, I later realised, always accompanied Alyosha, whether on the field or off it. Thereafter, Alyosha, single handed, went on to score 12 points in 5 minutes despite being guarded by 3 guys, all of whom were over 6 feet tall! And that was all the spur the team needed, led by Alyosha in the front and galvanised by his 'never give up' attitude to sports, we went on to win one of the most memorable matches played in National Law School till date.

Even now when I meet alumni from NLS, that match is still remembered fondly.

That day I learnt something from Alyosha; its not something I can describe or put to words, its just a cold confidence that I can carry with me wherever I go, that I can do anything I want, if I just try hard enough. I learnt from Alyosha that to be truly happy in life, you cant be scared of anything, be it new challenges, change or even examining your own potential. I Learnt from Alyosha that there is no need to offer excuses or be embarrassed if you fail while trying something new. And most importantly- Alyosha taught me how to live life, he taught me that there is no use being sad or worried when you cant help the circumstances you are in, he taught me that the most important thing I can do in life is to be happy for every moment that I am in it. I was a boy when I met him and I think its fair to say that he played a significant part in shaping the man that I am today and so, I am grateful that now I have this medal to remember him by and this medal shall be cherished, along with his everlasting memory.

Respectfully and most sincerely yours

Adhiraj Singh

sa vidya ya vimuktaye

Dear arun uncle,

I know its late in the day, and i know its rude and unfeeling to be this late, but i still cant bring myself to talk about alyosha, even to his parents. I came to law school from a small town, and knew nothing of the social niceties which is pretty much all this place has in terms of substance (if it may be reffered so) when i came here. Alyosha was someone who treated me like a brother, sometimes more than that, and cared to look beyond the veneer. In a way, i got over my handicaps in law school, but he was amongst the few peole (i can only think of two) who knew me, my weeknesses, my strengths, probably better than me. I never have considered him gone, we stay uncle, we dont die. Life is about stories and memories, and thats what human beings essentially are. No one can die beyond these. I never participated in any things related to his going because he actually dint go for me. i dont know, sometimes i doubted my feelings for his departed self, but i dont know, i really never felt it. He was a part of me. He was the most enlightening person who knew me, and who i knew. My first school had a motto, "sa vidya ya vimuktaye": that is knowledge which frees, so he was freed,,,he had his knowledge...he knew other things from before. i am not a parent, and i dont know what it means to be one, but i can understand what it might mean to lose someone who you saw as the sole extension of yourself in this ever so mundane world, but i dont feel he is dead, he lives, in me, and all those who knew him and continue to know him. The spirit of carelessness, freedom, which he embodied, lived and was so high in espousing that few can be anything but jealous of it, cannot be understood by all, but the most able. he dint need it. he went. i might be rambling uncle, but if it matters, alyosha lives in me, and anything might die, but he will not. with most respectful regards,

Devranjan Mishra

Alyosha...The boy with the smile on his face, humming a song, without any shoes on his feet. This is exactly how I will always remember him.

He was one of the few people, who had the conviction just to be himself. He never pretended or even tried to do things just to please others (when you think about it, why should he have done so, he was very likeable just by being himself).

The last time I saw him was before I was just leaving for Sydney for my LLM, he wished me luck, I wish I had done the same.

Wherever you are Alyosha, I hope that you are at peace; you will always be missed by all those who knew you

Daisy Recalls
October 12, 2007

Alyosha Kumar was one of those rare concoctions of talent that combined a brilliant mind with fine sportsmanship. Even as school kid, most wondered how he managed to excel in so many fields.

Nithin Shivshanker, Alyosha's classmate from Lawrence

Fear and Loathing in Law School
Last a week a friend of mine was stabbed to death in Bangalore.

He was not the kind of guy who would like mourning. So I shall not try to be too sappy. Furthermore, if you see my post on suicide, you will know that I do not consider death tragic. However, there are times when death can be brutally senseless.

I think I can remember four people who died in college– one smashed out of his mind hit a road railing on his bike, two suicides and another really messed up guy who O.D-ied on the street outside college. But I would lie if I said those people meant anything to me. And they were all practically suicides. You shook your head and continued with life.

Looking at a dead person's Orkut page is like seeing a ghost. It makes your hair stand on edge. Alyosha Kumar's tells me that he loved 'ridiculousness'.

Alyosha had a complex sense of humour. 'Ridiculousness' is the kind of word that describes his antics and jokes. But I loved to run into him on campus or in the hostel. He said and did spectacular things all the time. Some people considered him weird but to me he was without a doubt one of the bright sparks in law school. Amongst all the Fuglies in the world with their head up some Professor, Senior Advocate or Partner's ass, he kept a smile on my face.

He was a gifted defender at Football with great tackles. He was also a fantastic Basketball player. Alyosha was a supreme athlete and was tough as nails. Another quality extremely rare in college. But he wasn't some weird stupid jock. We mooted together and were part of a firm that put me on a Vienna team something I will be grateful to him for that till I die. He may not have topped his class but he had a fantastic legal brain along with wide-ranging eclectic interests including music and books.

That is just one of the most senseless things about this particular death. Alyosha was someone who was so full of life. A genuine character who can never ever be replaced.

There are so many events that conspired in his death.

For starters he was never supposed to be in Bangalore at that time.

In Law School, the student body is supposed to be responsible for its own discipline. Then, came along this guy who I compare to Greg Chapell, who decided that he needed control over the disciplinary mechanism in order to fix the 'wrong' students. Since then, it becomes the responsibility of Appointed Students to report people to the faculty for suspension or even rustication. Nazi informants or Prefects for 23 year olds. You decide.

So a fellow student got Alyosha suspended for three months extending his stay in Bangalore. I think for possessing marijuana or something like that. He was stabbed hours before he was supposed to leave Bangalore for good. There will blood on the hands the people responsible for holding Alyosha back no matter how unintentional or good intentioned their actions were. The person who snitched must think- what if..

Then, there's the present climate against non-Kannada speakers in Bangalore. My friends in Bangalore tell me that people are forever pissed off nowadays. Angry and itching for a fight. And Bangalore could rival Delhi when it comes to harassment of women especially once it gets dark. It is the only city I know that turns into a war/riot zone on New Year's eve with biker gangs roaming around or setting up road-blocks to create trouble.

Yes, South Indians are mistreated by North Indians. Agreed. Yes, there are a lot of losers from North India who bring their obtuseness to Bangalore. However, racism for whatever justification is still racism.

There is this trait in the Kannada movement, typified as the sort of treachery that is being exacted by the Gowda family (who are at the vanguard of the movement) on the BJP right now by not honouring the power-sharing agreement. This goes right down to the auto driver on the street and the petrol pump vendors. These are people who jeopardize the futures of their children by not teaching them English in schools or justifying and spreading xenophobia amongst their people and violence as a solution. And when H.D. Kumaraswami's son smashed a local restaurant (Empire) for not serving him food late at night, his excuse for signing a confessional police statement was that he could not read Kannada well!

And whatever is the solution to the spoiling of Bangalore's atmosphere by loose moral outsiders I would suggest that stabbing people to death is not the solution. Nobody deserves to be stabbed and die bleeding on the road no matter how reckless a life they lead.

Alyosha Kumar it was a pleasure to know you. My condolonces to your parents and family.

Ridiculousness. That's how I'd remember your sense of humour. Even your death, for that matter.

Posted by W.T.F. Ittabari Impressions of a fellow Law schoolite

If there was something I will always remember Alyosha for, it was the ability to make an impression on every single person he met, even if for a few seconds. Mediocrity or being common was not in his nature, and buddy, I'll always miss that side of you. I can't even begin to put in words the feelings I have experienced in the past few days....but i've gone through anger, rage, sadness and utter helplessness, and I still cannot fathom the experience completely to categorise my state of mind.

All I can say is that the world will miss someone who had the potential to really influence it, and we will years from now speculate about how he would have gone about doing that. I remember the days in Vizag, and the hours spent together on a basketball court or at home watching anything we could land our hand on. Our games on the days before the board exams, when we'd challenge each other on the course for the next exam during the game. And of course the awesome times in Delhi, where I was perpetually at Alyosha's place or him at mine.

Me and my friends here still remember your trip to Singapore when you visited me, and I shall cherish and celebrate these memories rather than try to forget them.
Alyosha can best be described as a no nonsense individual who lived life to the fullest and gave others a hard time when not doing the same! He taught me a lot about life and now I will ensure that I live the way he would have wanted me to.

We will all miss him dearly, but we will also keep him in our hearts and celebrate the person he was and all that he did for us. May your soul rest in peace. Take care Alyosha....

Love,

Ankit, A close buddy from NPS

Early Morning Cold Taxi
– from Mami, his roommate in the first year of law school

At 5.30 am, when many of my buddies were tottering into bed after pondering through the night over what Hecksher and Ohlin were on, Arun and I woke up to accomplish the same task. We staggered into the corridor, feeling that familiar-September feeling, of having holidays and festivals round the corner, and sang, almost together, "Early Morning Cold Taxi" in the same tuneless monotone.

"Dude, WHAT is this song?" I asked. I had been singing this same line – actually, it was more like poetry recital – for two whole days without knowing what it was, what it meant, or where I had heard it.
"Dementor keeps singing this…"

When he got up for that day, we asked him, "Dude, play us this song…"
And he did. For the rest of the year, Dement insisted that there was one place where The Who sang this tunelessly. Nevertheless, we were hooked – to Early Morning Cold Taxi, and to Dement.

And before every exam, till he end of my fifth year, if I felt unsure or jittery, I'd sing to myself,

3:36, it's cold, I know I'm growing old,
With life's best side on the downward slope,
It's in my own hands, I know I'll cope,

My girl's with me and all my friends can see.

Here I am again,
Early morning cold taxi.
Early morning cold taxi.

At every Western Music, the three of us would briefly contemplate singing Early Morning Cold Taxi – branded our room song (one that changed to Grab your balls like Michael Jackson when Geek moved in) – and Al would chicken out.

Singing was the only thing that I had even seen Al chicken out of – he took on Lizzy and her bouts of madness, ESPN-Star and it's hiring policies (when he went up to their office in Singapore and demanded that he be taken in as a commentator), much bigger opponents from Al-Ameen in every football match, and Jian Johnson's might in that last basketball game. All with the same passion, intensity and earnestness.

In his own words, "I can't stay quiet in the face of injustice."
***

Al was also the source of endless entertainment and conflict in our room. In the run up to the 2003 World Cup, Arun and I decided that we had to make that trip to South Africa. And like all reasonable persons, we realised that the easiest way to do that would be through the "Britannia Khao, World Cup Jao" scheme. And like good boys who didn't overspend, we bought one pack of biscuits a day, and religiously saved the wrappers. When we had enough points to be eligible for the trip to the World Cup, we rushed back to the room to pick up the other wrappers and claim the hallowed Scratch Card.

When we reached the room, we found it spotlessly clean – even my extra-messy cubicle was swept and swabbed, the clothes were all folded and kept in the cupboard, and the wrappers were missing. Al had cleaned up our room, and cringed at the fact that his two roommates ate these cream biscuits everyday, and had not even bothered to throw away the wrappers. We didn't talk to Al for two whole days.

And his response was typically Al, "You guys don't love me."

We do, Al. And we always did.
***

There are so many enduring things, incidents and quirks about Al – like how he used to study really hard way before the exam, and potter around on the day before it, and go for a long run or jump and try hit the ceiling. Like how he was mortified of frogs.

I shall be eternally grateful to Al for one thing – teaching me how to play FIFA. I used to play FIFA even before I met Al, but he was the one who taught me how to play FIFA. And when I'd play for a little too long on his computer at night, and moan and curse loudly while he tried to get some sleep, he'd always tell me, "Mami man, hump off."

Once more, Al, just ask me to 'hump off', and I'll stop playing FIFA forever.
***

"This world was never meant for one as beautiful as you."
– Don McLean

Swaroop

19

Emails – From Family

Friends

Translation of Russian

With Alyosha's father, Arun Kumar, I am familiar more than 25 years. Once, at one or our meetings, we spoke about our families. And he told me, when he was in long business trip in Vladivostok with his wife — Deepa, the son who was given Russian name - Alyosha - was born. This story actually touched me. It is absolutely extraordinary case - Indian boy was given Russian name. During all my further meetings with Arun I was always interested about Alyosha, his relations with classmates and friends in India and his plans for his future life. During my meetings with Arun I always felt his love to the son. As a father he was proud of his son's achievements in study and in life.

My meeting with Alyosha took place once during New Year's vacation of 2007 when he arrived to Moscow. I couldn't miss this chance and invited Arun with Alyosha to visit my house. Russians believe that the first impression is the most sincere. When they entered my house, I saw a very handsome young man, with open face, radiating self-confidence and respectability.

— 1 —

С отцом Алёши, Аруном Кумаром, я знаком более 25 лет. Однажды, при очередной встрече, мы разговорились о своих семьях. Он рассказал, что когда он был в длительной спецкомандировке во Владивостоке у них с Дели родился сын, которому дали русское имя Алёша. Этот рассказ меня очень тронул, т.к. совсем не ординарный случай—индийскому малышу дали русское имя. При встречах с Аруном я всегда интересовался об Алёше, как у него складывались отношения со своими сверстниками в Индии, кем он хотел стать в жизни. По рассказам Аруна я чувствовал его любовь к сыну, как он гордился его достижениями в учёбе и жизни.

Моя встреча с Алёшей состоялась в Новогодние каникулы 2007, когда он прилетел в Москву. Я не мог не использовать этот случай и пригласил Аруна с Алексеем посетить мой дом. Как у нас говорят первое впечатление - самое искреннее. Когда он вошёл, я увидел красивого молодого человека, с открытым лицом, излучающим уверенность в себе, добропорядочность и спокойствие.

В ходе этой встречи с друзьями мне удалось уединиться с Алёшей, т.к. мне очень хотелось ближе познакомиться с ним, узнать его жизненные интересы, его взгляд на будущее. Наша беседа длилась более часа

Continued... on Next page

блестал английский, мы оба хорошо
понесла ли друг друга. Мы говорили на
разные темы: он интересовал расспрашивал
о России, о Москве, о Россий...-Индийско
дружбе, и её практических примерах.
   В ходе нашей беседы я увидел в Алёше
зрелого мужчину, с широким кругозором знаний
по различным направлениям, чувствовалось что
он много читает литературы, и будучи выпускник
юридического института глубоко понимает проблемы
развития государства как по политическим, так
и экономическим, и социальным направлениям.
А ведь ему тогда было всего 22 года.
   Я глубоко и искренне соболезную Анджу
и Дели за трагическую и безвременную
утрату сына, и я убеждён, что в лице Алёши
Индия потеряла достойного гражданина страны.
Вечная ему память.
                                    Г.М. Шаварин.

During this meeting I managed to spend some time with Alyosha, because I actually wanted to talk to him, to know him better. To learn his vital interests, his views of the future. Our conversation lasted more than an hour, though he didn't know Russian and I was not good enough in English. But we understood each other very well.

We spoke on different subjects: he asked about Russia, Moscow, Russian-Indian relationship and friendship.

During our conversation I realized that Alyosha was the mature man, with a broad outlook and knowledge of various aspects, felt that he read a lot, and being the graduate of the institute, where he studied law, deeply understood problems of development of the state, like in political, and in economical and social spheres. At that very time he was only 22 years old.

I deeply and sincerely condole Arun and to Deeps in tragic and untimely loss of their son, and I am convinced that India lost the worthy citizen of the country. Our memory about Alyosha Kumar will be with us forever.
GM Shavin

Greetings for Onam

Dear Arun & Deepa (I take the liberty of dispensing with the Mr & Mrs)

Thank you so much for remembering us at Onam. As a Mallu, will you believe that I have never been in Kerala during this season? However I am fascinated by the festival because of the secular connotations it has. We celebrate it at Chaitanya School precisely for this reason and, among others as a learning experience of our diversity. As Shubha is always reminding me, we are Third Culture Kids – born and bred outside the native place, educated elsewhere and with a karma bhumi even further away!!

Thank you for reading my blog. It has been put together rather haphazardly with pieces jotted down long ago, only some of which have been published. May I take the liberty of clarifying that I am in absolute agreement with you that we should not wear our religion on our shirt sleeves. That is exactly what I am trying to say, that we may worship any God, whatever or however we conceive him to be. That is entirely a private matter and has NO bearing on the way we look or how we dress. That is why I resent it when people comment on my Religion, when they are actually referring to my accoutrements or racial characteristics!!

It must have been a poignant moment to receive Alyosha's Law degree, a fulfilling of his years of hard work and sincerity. It is good to know that the Trust has achieved its goals for the first year. We are grateful for the sponsorship of Komal's education this year. I am amazed at how a chance conversation between my daughter and a fellow passenger can touch the life of needy young Komal in such a beneficial manner.

I am sorry for taking so long to reply, but I wanted to ponder over many of the thoughts you put down, mainly because they have crossed my mind as well.

Like you I also feel that the lack of foundation in a proper Primary Education is the cause of shaky personality edifices in adulthood. At Chaitanya (Forgive me for reverting to it- it is a mission and a vision all rolled into one for me) our motto is Childhood for the Child, because we do believe that the Child IS the father of the man, and we need to make sure that we give him a solid foundation of values and principles, dispel ignorance at a grass-root level, and make sure that he gets equal opportunities on a level playing field, as far as possible. I think Alyosha was a visionary to have mulled over these thoughts at such a young age, but the fact that he had a home where he could discuss such matters speaks volumes of the kind of parents you were. Homes like yours are the need of the hour, and we need to replicate them in society, to spread the message of tolerance and non-violence.

Shubha forwarded the pictures of your family, and I'm grateful to technology that memories of happier times have been encapsulated in those photographs, and that they can be shared with us.

We shall never have an answer to the eternally asked," why do bad things happen to good people", but Alyosha's tragic demise seems to have set in motion so many admirable activities – your Trust in his memory, the coming together of so many like-minded people, and above all a yearning all around for a better world. Perhaps God in his Heaven wanted to use a pure soul like Alyosha as a conduit, although it is poor consolation at a personal level. I can't think of a more admirable way than what Deepa and you have done to condone Society for its mindless, dastardly acts. You have proved to all of us that " ....with all its sham, drudgery and broken dreams, it is still a beautiful world" – A world Alyosha would be proud of.

With regards
Elizabeth Koshy
22 Sept 2008

Tribute from an uncle

My Dear Arun,

The more I think about this clossal tragedy, the unbearable loss of dear Alyosha the more I think of the ways of destiny.

Why is it that nature or destiny if you will is so unkind to the very world it creates by taking away the best it first gives. It takes away the best sooner than others. I see it so often. Our Alyosha was no ordinary young man. His exceptional intellect was an investment in India's future. It pains me even more when I realize, and I wonder, if everyone appreciates, that in him we as Indians have lost someone who would have contributed to the good of our nation with his intellect and maturity.

I recollect him from his childhood days. All parents are proud of their children. Each of us is. I am. And yet when we saw the sparks of maturity and brilliance even at that young age we all knew here was a young man who would be brilliant and out shine others. Seeing this I recollect how Deepa would buy all the intellectually stimulating and challenging toys and books for him and he would soon be beyond those hungry for more knowledge. Was there another kid who had the general knowledge like him? I don't recollect any one.

You may have forgotten, but I remember I would play football with the kids in Dhanraj Mahal. He was much younger than Raj and Kiran and yet would ask me if he could play. Of course I said yes, and was ready to see he was not pushed (being young), but he stood his ground. He took to sports like his father (you). Then I moved away, but never stopped hearing how well he was doing. I was not in the least surprised when he joined the best Law School. He could have picked any field and been selected and excelled.

I regret I never met him in these past few years. I was so happy when Deepa and you came to US and I could ask you about Alyosha. That he was graduating and soon headed for a law apprenticeship was a source of joy. I was waiting to see the brilliant attorney blossom. How unkind God can be some times. He is gone, but his memory is a source of inspiration, even for us elders. How much he learnt and how he matured in his given few years on this earth.

Arun I salute you and Deepa for bringing up such a brilliant young star and I pray that God All Mighty grants you all the courage and wisdom to bear this unbearable loss.

My friend I am with you both in your grief.
Sincerely,

IJ Arora
October 9, 2007

A jewel is lost

For those of us who are past our prime it is difficult to believe that a flower which had not even fully blossomed has been snatched away from us. If it is not the cruelty of fate what else could it be? When I think of Alyosha the picture which appears before my eyes is of a young handsome boy, full of life, so mature yet seemingly so care free. When I met him last in a wedding reception I jokingly remarked," So, Alyosha! You would soon be a great lawyer". He promptly retorted" Uncle! Firstly it won't be too soon because it is time I started working and secondly, for you all I would continue to be a small boy."

Well! That was Alyosha. Frank, candid yet downright humble. Unless one knew him closely one was likely to misinterpret his forthrightness for arrogance. He was extremely independent in his thought and action. For example he would never let anyone else run any chores for him. He believed in doing everything himself.

Having known him since the time he was born (yes because

we were all together in the thick Vladivostok winter) and closely seen him growing in to a fine young man, there are many memorable moments which one could now painfully recall. But there is one particular moment which appears before my eyes. When he was born he with his chinky eyes stole every Russians heart in the hospital. For some reasons he and Deepa underwent a long period of hospitalization. During this time he got used to being cared by different people. So when he and Deepa came home, he was friendly with every one and would easily go in to any body's lap. Soon he won every one's heart.

On a hind sight one can say that he was a darling of every one when he came to this world and he left the world as a darling of all those who knew him.

RK Sharma
October 8, 2007

20

The Brave New World

Foundation

Alyosha was a very intelligent, compassionate and humane person, who always expressed his views with conviction and without fear or favour. He would stick his neck out to fight injustice – often at great personal cost.

His parents and well-wishers, in pursuance of Alyosha' desire, have set up a public charitable trust, "The Brave New World Foundation", a truly befitting tribute to Alyosha's life and the values he stood for.

Objectives

[a] The advancement or promotion of education and learning in all its branches in such manner as the trustees may think fit including :-
(i) Awarding scholarships, freeships or otherwise and cash payments to poor persons and widows desirous of receiving primary, secondary and higher education in India or abroad, as also providing books, uniforms and such other

educational assistance as students may require;

(ii) Awarding Scholarship in India and Fellowships and grants by way of loan or otherwise and on such terms and conditions as the Trustees may think fit for the purposes of undertaking, prosecuting and encouraging research work in any branch of Law, Engineering, Medicine or any other branch or branches of modern applied science in its widest and more comprehensive sense;

(iii) Establishment and support of Professorship, Fellowships, Lectureships, Scholarships and prizes at any School, College or other Educational Institutions;

(iv) To undertake research in any field and / or make payment to any University, College, Association or Institution to be used for research in any field. Establishment and / or acquisition and maintenance and / or support of School, Colleges, Vocational / Educational Guidance and Counseling Bureaus, Students Hostels, Study Centers, Research Centers, Universities and other Institutions or Funds for imparting education and training of students;

(v) Organising group training in any trade or vocation;

(vi) Providing vocational/educational guidance and counseling and/or establishing, supporting, conducting Vocational Guidance Bureau;

(vii) Establishment, maintenance and support of libraries, museums and reading rooms for advancement or education and knowledge;

(viii) To undertake, carry out, promote and sponsor any activity for publication of any books, literature, newspapers, etc. or for organising lectures or seminars likely to advance the objects or for giving merit awards, scholarships, loans or any other assistance to deserving students or other scholars or persons to enable them to prosecute their studies or academic pursuits or researches;

(ix) Establish Hostels and other staying facilities for the students of schools, colleges and other educational course institutions.

(x) Grant of endowments at Universities, Research Institutions and other Educational Medical and Scientific Institutions (whether now existing or hereinafter established) for spread of education and knowledge in all or any branches;

(xi) Establishment and maintenance of and support Hostels and / or Boarding Houses and grant of free boarding and loading to poor and deserving students upon such terms and for such period in each case as the Trustees may deem fit;

[b] Providing medical relief in such manner as the Trustees may think fit including :-

(i) (Grant, subscriptions and donations to hospitals, dispensaries, convalescent homes, Asylums, Nursing Homes, Health and Medical Centres and other public and/or private institutions administering medical relief upon such terms and conditions and for such period as the Trustees may think fit;

(ii) Grant of medical help to the poor and deserving persons during epidemic, famine, flood, earthquake or any unforeseen calamity or war or war like operation, riots, civil commotions and similar occurrences.

(iii) Distribute free medicines, organize blood donation camps, eye camps, doctor consultations and all related services for better health and nutrition facilities.

[c] Providing relief of poverty and/or distress by helping persons who are poor and needy, deserving or charitable help by :-

(i) Distribution of free food and clothing to the poor and needy;

(ii) Setting up or helping by endowment or otherwise orphanage or poor houses for the benefit of orphans and/or other deserving persons and destitutes;

(iii) Setting up or helping by endowments or otherwise institutions or funds for the benefit of poor widows;

(iv) Establishing or rendering help to any institutions or fund for the alleviation of sufferings;

(v) To establish, run, support, work centres for women, destitutes, handicapped, poor and needy people for providing employment or to collaborate with other trusts, centres institutions carrying on similar activities.

[d] Advancement of any other object of general public utility not involving the carrying on of any activity for profit :-

(i) Creation, maintenance, supply or support of gardens, gymnasiums, physical culture centres and other means of public recreation and advancement of health and hygiene.

(ii) To undertake any programme of rural development

(iii) To assist in the execution and promotion of a programme which the Trust can lawfully carry either directly or through any agency or any person or persons or in any other manners.

(iv) To undertake, carry out, promote and sponsor or assist activity for the promotion and growth of the national economy.

[e] To enter into any arrangement, agreement, understanding with any other trust, company, firm or body for the purpose of effectively conducting the affairs of the Trust and giving effect to the objects of the Trust.

Gold Medal instituted on Alyosha's Name at National Law School.

To donate to **The Brave New World Foundation**,

Contact: The Brave New World Foundation
      3A New Shiv Sadan
      L.J. Cross road No. 2
      Mahim (West) ,
      Mumbai – 400016

TELEPHONE: +91-22-24442154, +91-22-24440366 (Telefax), +91-9819096915
Website: **www.thebravenewworldfoundation.org**
Email: **thebravenewworldfoundation@gmail.com**
Facebook:
www.facebook.com/thebravenewworldfoundation

ABOUT CMDE ARUN KUMAR (RETD)

Cmde Arun Kumar (Retd). Cmde Arun has had a distinguished career of 31 years in the Navy. He was commissioned into the Navy on 01 Jul 1973 after having graduated from NDA [41st Course]. Soon after obtaining his Watchkeeping certificate, he joined the Submarine Arm in 1975. He topped his submarine course in 1976 and obtained his Dived Watchkeeping Certifacte soon thereafter. During his 28 years in submarines, he held various staff and Command appointments. He topped his SM COQC(Perishers).

His Commands include two kilo class subs viz; Sindhuraj & Sindhughosh, Submarine Base Captain and Capt SM 10 (Sqn captain Shishumar Class), INS Virbahu & COMCOS (E), guided missile destroyer Rajput, Submarine Training School Satavahana. His last appointment was PDSMAQ at NHQ where he steered submarine projects of strategic importance to the Arm in particular and the Navy in General. He is a specialist Navigator, wherein he topped the course in 1980. He has also attended the Staff Course at DSSC and the Naval Higher Command Course. He was part of the Commissioning crew as First Lieutenant of IN's first SSGN Chakra and formulated its SOPs. He was decorated twice by the President of India for his devoted and distinguished services with Nao Sena Medal (NM) in 1991 and Ati Vishisht Seva Medal(AVSM) in 2003. He took premature retirement in 2004.

www.ingramcontent.com/pod-product-compliance
Lightning Source LLC
Chambersburg PA
CBHW060742050426
42449CB00008B/1289